Rel. Life

HOLINESS AND RADICALISM
IN RELIGIOUS LIFE

HOLINESS AND RADICALISM
IN RELIGIOUS LIFE

THOMAS F. O'MEARA, O.P.

HERDER AND HERDER

1970
HERDER AND HERDER NEW YORK
232 Madison Avenue, New York 10016

Portions of two chapters of this book appeared in different form in *Sisters Today,* 40 (March 1969) and *Review for Religious,* 28 (July, 1969).

Revisores Ordinis: Cletus J. Wessels, O.P., Mark Scannell, O.P.
Imprimi Potest: Clement Collins, O.P., Provincial
Nihil Obstat: Cletus J. Wessels, O.P.
Imprimatur: ✠James J. Byrne, Archbishop of Dubuque

Library of Congress Catalog Number: 72–110794
© 1970 by Herder and Herder, Inc.
Manufactured in the United States

Contents

We ourselves must change to master change.
We must rethink all our old ideas and
beliefs before they capture and destroy us.

Robert Francis Kennedy

Preface

In America the renewal of religious life began before Vatican II. The Council gave it an unexpected freedom and dynamism. But a definitive renewal, proud, calm, aglow with newness, never appeared. Today, after less than a decade and after innumerable changes, religious life is in more of a crisis than ever. Both its present and its future are challenged, and few religious can look at their past without emotion. Renewal has not produced a new era of religious life or a new type of religious life, but seems to have been only the first stage of a process yet unknown. One main aspect of renewal was the actual collapse of a great deal of what had been the life of a sister, brother, or religious priest. Daniel Callahan writes:

There can no longer be any doubt that the Church has entered into a period of profound confusion and disorientation. Far from curing us of all our ills, the Second Vatican Council succeeded mainly in revealing how deep-seated are the problems of contemporary Christianity. To be sure, the Council accomplished many valuable things. . . .

What is surprising is the way the concern over "implementation" has given way, in many quarters, to concern over far more basic issues of Christian existence. Even if Christianity were renewed, would it have a future? Who is God? What, if anything, does the traditional doctrine of God—or of man, or of the Church, or of the supernatural—have to say to contemporary man? One might call questions like these pre-institutional.[1]

[1] Daniel Callahan, "Foreword," to Rosemary Haughton, *The Transformation of Man* (Springfield, 1967), p. 3.

ix

The purpose of the following pages is to ask whether renewal in the religious life must not be replaced by radicalism. Did not, really, this first, unsatisfactory, and somewhat destructive period serve only to introduce more radical demands? These demands are similar to other times—those of Benedict and Dominic and Francis, and of Ignatius Loyola. In their Christian and social force they are truly radical. *Whereas renewal is the elaboration and updating of the structures of religious life already in existence, radicalism begins with the root demands of being a Christian, and living in a Christian apostolic community.* Renewal is baffled when its improvements lead only to more clamor and dissatisfaction; radicalism begins from below and, in the Christian revolutionary spirit of faith and hope, allows every structure which is not of the gospel or the Spirit to be questioned and to be (if this is best) replaced.

This book is not a work of theological research. It is based greatly on experience. As a life, the religious life is something to be lived. Life is lived in the present in the midst of other men and women. Religious life will exist tomorrow only because *we* are discovering and living it today. Some knowledge of the charismatic beginnings of the followers of Bruno or Vincent de Paul is important; a study of the decline and renewal of the great orders is always instructive, although these lessons have rarely been heeded by authorities; meditation on vocation and following, life and ministry in the New Testament is basic, and here especially, scholarship gives birth to new life. This book is to a great extent a reflective gathering of what I have lived through in the past five years. I explicitly do not take credit for many of the ideas contained in it. I learned them from many conversations with sisters deeply concerned and hard at work in the renewal of their congregations. Above all, I learned them by living through an exciting and frustrating period in the Midwestern province of Dominicans. In a relatively short time I encountered a tremendous amount of courage, talent, and dedication. It became possible to live the religious life unashamedly before the New Testament and before the demands of apostolic efficacy in the real world. This was always experienced as a communal effort. Joined to intelligence and creativity was a certain *joie de vivre*. Perhaps creative joy *is* religious life. Naturally, there was also condemnation and oscillation, fear and escapism, and that strange preference for death and destruction over the demands of change. This is what religious life is not.

Finally, I had excellent tutors for this discovery of life: young Dominicans. No one knows exactly what radicalism in religious life is, or what new community styles will be. But what I have learned I have learned mainly from those younger than myself. For thanks and acknowledgment let me single out only a few as representative of many others: George Doherty, Neil Wise, Mark Scannell, . . . and communities as disparate as Dubuque and Houston, Paris and La Paz. ·

Thomas Franklin O'Meara, O.P.

HOLINESS AND RADICALISM
IN RELIGIOUS LIFE

1. Renewal or Radicalism?

The Catholic Church exists in the midst of not one but many revolutions. There is liturgical creativity as well as a complex struggle over authority. Intramural struggles have broadened into secular social problems. The Berrigans tell us that prison is the ideal place for worship, and that bishops should join them there. Marshall McLuhan describes how the electronic revolution is changing our minds, causing polarization and destruction, yet beckoning to union in the mystical Body of Christ.

RENEWAL OR RADICALISM?

A renewal of religious life began in America in the 1950's. It was given freedom and impetus with Vatican II, although it is not the most important of the post-conciliar revolutions. Theoretically, the Catholic Church can exist without specially dedicated communities of men and women called "religious," although the history and efficacy of any Christian church might challenge whether this situation has ever existed or should exist. The struggle, however, of the orders and congregations to face simultaneously a multitude of problems has a wider significance. In the renewal of religious life there comes together most of the wider problems present in the renewal of every church for the 1970's. There is the problem of authority vis-à-vis the demands of freedom and creative response to a new society; there is

1

the search for meaningful community which has an integral mission and a dynamic liturgy. Apostolic problems as diversified as racial equality and the solution to a thirteen-billion-dollar educational system form the visible external framework. Finally, religious problems emerging from or endemic to our society, such as the puzzling uncertainty over a new approach to God and personal prayer, are here intensified.

From another point of view, the opening of the life of a Jesuit, a Franciscan, or a Benedictine to contemporary American society reveals many of the problems facing religious to be the same problems facing American families and students. What kind of community or familial life can replace this gnawing alienation I feel within myself, even when I am most successful? How can I prepare myself so that in the future I will not inevitably become a fearful voice of reaction?

The purpose of the following pages is not to offer a discussion of the problems of sister-renewal or constitution-updating in the style of the past ten years. Since Vatican II we have learned to speak of the *renewal* of the religious life. Yet, most religious—especially if they are unhampered by being administrators—would testify that after five to ten years of this the situation, whether it is theoretically worse or better, is definitely more desperate. The reason for this, briefly, is that freedom and hope of improvement open up ever more vistas. The religious life has to replace centuries of static preservation, and this will take more than five years. Secondly, the age in which we live is one of the radically and multiple new; a mentality exists where any enterprise is questioned. Finally, this is one of the four or five great revolutionary times of history since Jesus Christ. The conquest of the moon is only a symbol. The work of the Christian theologian or teacher has been radically changed by inexpensive jet travel and by systems of computers and television. Our daily life is a constant probe—in the form of a question mark about the future.

2

We will return to look more carefully at American society. These few initial remarks allow us to realize that an easy renewal of the religious life is not sufficient. It was only the first stage which having been successfully implemented leads us to the impasse where we now find ourselves. Improving the religious life—in a way undreamt of ten years ago—has not diminished the frustration and the uncertainty. Renewal must yield to radicalism. The word *radicalism* is chosen rather than revolution, since it is still uncertain what kind or degree of revolution—a real turning upside down of things to find the new—would be necessary. Radicalism means getting to the roots, to the roots of Christian community life and apostolate. It recognizes two radical sources: the New Testament and the situation of today. It learns from the half-dozen great figures of religious life, but owes allegiance only to Christ and to our times. Radicalism is chosen because only the freedom to think radically about the future of religious life can serve as the climate in which to master the most severe doubts about its future. "Radicalism," with its allusion to radical politics, is chosen intentionally, for it is becoming increasingly clear in the American social and political domain that some radical solutions are necessary for American society. Tom Hayden, founder of the SDS, writes, explaining the radical approach: "The radical style, on the other hand, takes as its presupposition Dewey's claim that we are free to the extent that we know what we are about. Radicalism as a style presumes a willingness to continually press forward the query: Why? Radicalism finds no rest in conclusions; answers are seen as provisional, to be discarded in the face of new evidence or changed conditions."[1]

[1] "A Letter to the New Left," *The New Student Left,* M. Cohen and D. Hale, editors (Boston, 1967), p. 6. "The first effort, then, should be to state a vision: What is the perimeter of human possibility in this epoch?" *Ibid.,* p. 16. "When this Administration completes its term, the United States is likely to have more social problems than now, more racism, more urban deterioration. In saying this, I do not picture Richard

3

American Religious Life

It would be interesting and instructive to trace the history of the religious life in the United States, not in those lengthy and quasi-mythical biographies of nineteenth-century worthies, but in the encounter of secular and religious lifestyles. With some exceptions the American experience had minimal influence on the religious life. Some groups such as Mother Seton's were born out of the turmoil of American history; other groups such as the Dominicans in Kentucky and the Jesuits in Georgetown were once on the way to becoming American expressions of an Order. However, as with many things in the American Church, the religious life was strongly bound to the central administration of the Catholic Church. By the early nineteenth century there was little trace of an authentic American style of religious life. In fact, just the opposite was the norm. Some of the most observant forms in the world of French Trappist or Carmelite life could be found in the United States, even more rigorous in the observance of constitutions than their European confreres who were determining the legislation. Women in the religious life made the attempts to establish groups of distinctively American communities responding to American apostolates, but these were modified by strong ties to their male counterparts or by legalistic administration in Rome. Yet the religious life flourished in the United States, flourished so greatly that its explosion in quantity and quality in the past twenty years gives it a unique and permanent place in the history of American ecclesial institutions. The lasting question is why and how so many Americans entered forms of the religious life which were alien to their American way of life. There was, correspondingly, a high

---

Nixon as some kind of rightist demon but as a moderate conservative in a time when basic problems cannot be solved without radical departures." Michael Harrington, *Toward a Democratic Left* (Baltimore, 1968), p. 285.

4

toll: damage to personalities, the rejection of creative and inventive people. Still, it is now clear that these tens of thousands of Americans did not lose their basic pragmatism or common sense, for when the opportunity came to challenge European and medieval institutions, an enormous amount of psychological pressure came forth with a vengeance.

Before we turn to the period surrounding Vatican II, let us continue this brief comparison of religious life and American experience. Convents and monasteries lived an institutionalized schizophrenia. George Santayana could write: "America did not have to wait for its present universities with their departments of academic philosophy, in order to possess a living philosophy— to have a distinct vision of the universe and definite convictions about human destiny."[2] Religious institutions housed Americans, and worked successfully at attracting hundreds of young men and women who existed to preach or teach in America. Still, the life was officially devoid of anything American. A careful and almost enthusiastic cult of the old, whether that of nineteenth-century France or thirteenth-century Spain, held sway. The further a person went in excluding "the world," the better he was. Any student of psychology (or of Aquinas, for that matter—whose "grace perfects Nature") could see that this was dangerously divisive. Most religious have experienced this strange quest of the medieval or the European, and many difficulties today stem from the long-term neglect of American experience. Only the pressure of this past dichotomy can explain the speed with which some responded to its breakdown. Waking up and realizing that the burdens of thirteenth-century monastic life in Colgone no longer hovered near with the vengeful spirit was a truly eschatological experience for many religious. It became shockingly clear that much of this past ossification had no worthwhile connection with either following the gospel or

---

[2] George Santayana, *Winds of Doctrine: Studies in Contemporary Opinion* (New York), pp. 186–187.

5

ministering effectively to fellow Americans. There is a certain echo of Martin Luther King's "Free, free at last!"

And yet for others these past structures were faith itself. Big or small changes—all were unacceptable because they struck at a hallowed monoform structure. Men and women appeared to have identified totally with this alien system. Had they really? Perhaps in their own way they remained Americans. Some chose a very severe "contemplative" direction where intensity of faith and grace overcame many obstacles and did much good, and in this sense they were a witness of the Transcendent to the turmoil of American life. Others, many of whom most severely defended the values of their own tradition and who were reluctant to miss exercises, etc., did compromise. They developed a certain second life, not an apostolic endeavor but a communal substitute. They became interested in a certain glamour which their own, frequently poor families could not provide; they took pride in a class of friends, in the ability to raise money, in administrative and ecclesiastical positions. For this latter group, now precisely as this endeavor reaches its fruition, values have reversed themselves; it has become the wrong thing, the disgraceful thing to be part of certain political and business establishments. It is no longer fulfilling but dangerous to be the chief administrator of a school. The action has moved elsewhere as American changes.

The great innovations of Vatican II began in Europe. Europe desperately needed a council like Vatican II and had been preparing for it since 1945. There was recognition of the widespread dechristianization in France, Belgium, Austria, and Germany. The religious life in France was challenged by proposals that cities were mission territories to be served by worker priests. Europe's response was unique and ultimately unsatisfactory. The basic mode of religious life was retained with habit, communal worship, and discipline, while outside the religious house a large amount of leeway was given. This approach exercised almost no influence towards a radical renewal of a

6

particular group or way of life; rather it introduced a new form of the seemingly omnipresent divided personality of religious life, which we saw already existed in America. Two or more life-styles were combined, alternating with each other for different circumstances. This helps to explain how, for example, the French Dominicans, could be living in an extremely monastic atmosphere at some hours and wearing black sweaters and working with Communists at other hours.

If by widespread renewal of religious life we mean a real open theological and encompassing study and effort at improving this way of life, it began with the various renewal movements among sisters in the United States. We can fill out a history of this by reading the reports of the various Notre Dame conferences.[3] Into this modest movement Vatican II broke, announcing that among its many tasks would be the *aggiornamento* of religious life throughout the world. This was only a secondary effort of the Council, but it was necessary if the Council was to attain a real pastoral renewal, for the tone and execution of a great deal of the Church's mission is in the hands of religious. The underlying thrust of this conciliar renewal was mainly the application of other conciliar insights to religious life. Among them we might cite: a positive attitude towards the process of secularization and the values of human society; an allowance of creative adaptation of the liturgy to particular times and situations; the recognition of the presence of grace throughout the world—in other Christian communities, in the world religions, in mission lands, in non-believers, in the deepest aspirations of the world—and hence a revitalization and expansion of the mission of the Church. These currents, and above all the recognition of the multiple and untiring presence of Christ and his grace in the world, unleashed the contemporary crises and changes in religious life. The *Decree on the Appropriate Re-*

[3] See the various publications of the Notre Dame Sisters' Institutes of Spirituality, beginning in 1953.

newal of the Religious Life was simply a modest channeling of their impetus. This is substantiated by the inability of "new" constitutions to channel or stem the tide of renewal, and by our realization that religious life will never again in this century be developed only along the lines of law. In all of this, religious life is simply typical of what happened generally at the Council. Underlying theological ideas unleashed a wave of questioning, change, dissatisfaction, and more change. When the documents were written Catholics still lived in the age of ecclesiastical law; when the Council ended that lengthy era had been replaced by a Christian critical creativity which struggled to be evangelical and relevant. There are many commentaries on Vatican II's decree on the updating of religious life; there is no need to write another one here. We should, however, observe that (like most conciliar documents) it contains *radical principles extending beyond renewal* to the severe questioning of religious structures. Two of these principles come immediately to mind: emphasis on the gospel and the taking of utility, simplicity, contemporaneity (the famous "signs of the times") as matrices for religious life. Actually, everything lasting in the document is based upon these two catalysts. This is not surprising since the mission of the Church as well as of theology is an activity oscillating between two poles: the event and commission of Jesus Christ and the particular society where it is to be lived and preached.

What Is Happening to Renewal?

Vatican II spoke constantly of the renewal of the Church. It is clear—from a perusing of *The National Catholic Reporter*—that renewal both did and did not happen. Shortly after, the Council renewal was seen to be open-ended rather than closed. It was not sufficient to put the letter of the conciliar documents into practice and relax, although a few dioceses and religious congregations did this. Rather the Council had done what Pope John first said it would: it opened things up. And things remained open. The catalytic principles within the conciliar texts were not to be stifled by a legalistic implementation; rather they were lights showing new roads to be built into the future. Renewal could not mean only the revivification, the renewing, the re-establishing of something from the past. Rather it meant searching for the new as a solution for the inadequacies of the present, inadequacies born mainly of the relatively immediate past.

In order to compare renewal with a more radical openness to the problems of religious life we must look for a moment at the progress of renewal in religious life. It has centered mainly around the rewriting of constitutions. The outcome is always dubious when Christians start "renewing" their institutions by rewriting laws and creeds. The momentum of Christianity as well as of the great movements in Church history comes from freedom, from a new challenge, and from a particular need in a new time. Meetings with the purpose of solving problems entirely through legislation and administration can only fail. Renewal itself took on a very legal character in the months after the Council. A great deal of effort was spent on constitutions, laws, new kinds of elections, narrow elections of new people. Relatively little time was spent on listening to the real (hence radical) needs of the world, on reassessment, on introducing new ways of living together. Renewal was effected *within* the same basic social and political framework that had governed the religious to that moment. Although many were unhappy with the structures of religious life, many others clung to them and their political power as the only hope. Consequently, the renewal of religious life, rather than becoming a community search for the exciting and important, centered around political power. More important, this political power was allowed to exist and function *only* within the old structure. This struggle between the maxi-

9

malists and minimalists of constitutional and legal change was hopeless; on these terms the liberal and open direction was closed from the start. For constitutional and legislative meetings (once the charismatic Founding Fathers are dead) are notoriously slow and unimaginative. Democracy (and even this was only imperfectly present) is not an apt system for radical renewal. Once it was granted that the future of religious life should be determined within the framework of political activity set up in the past, it was doomed to frustration.

Four stages appear in the past and on-going renewal of religious life. Their chronological appearance is the exact *opposite* of what their order should be. These four levels of renewal are applicable to the wider scene, true of the renewal of any aspect of the Church, and of the challenge to renewal facing our universities, suburbs, cities and political parties. *The four stages are: legal, theological, social, psychological.* We have noted that the renewal of religious life began with law. It should have begun with the psychological make-up of the people involved. Next, it should have progressed to a free, complete, outside evaluation through management consultant techniques of all institutions, structures, and programs. Then it should have asked about the theological inspiration and tradition of religious life. Finally, all this would have found its implementation in new structures for personnel and management, for community and apostolate with a minimum of legislation. We know that the opposite course was chosen, is still being chosen throughout the Church and society. Its effects are half-way measures, polarization, losses, and unnecessary risks.

The first step of religious renewal should be to question the structures within which renewal will be done. Only those few groups which really allowed widespread participation and which radically minimalized all superiors succeeded in opening themselves up to future possibilities. This does not imply that all the structures of the past are a burden. But the re-introduction (I avoid the word *preservation;* most structures which people have to work to preserve are not worth it) of a more evangelical and realistic religious life must begin by at least calling into question past political structures. A religious group can be "renewed" without doing this; but it cannot face radical challenge as long as its structural presuppositions are unchallenged. Remaining within the same legal and political framework excludes radicalism, since it implies that radicalism is not necessary. (Complementing Mother General with appointed Provincials is not changing structure; it is modifying an existing one. Radicalism seriously questions whether either have any value today.)

This emphasis upon renewal through laws and the unchallenged retention of most past structures gives a wrong sense of priorities. It implies that the crisis faces the administration of the religious group. This is not true. The crisis faces *the people* in religious life. The decline of novices is not due to lack of funds for vocational literature; it is due to the fact that such literature and the entire concept is now meaningless. People do not leave the religious life because their letters are not answered efficiently; they leave because they are answered inhumanly. The crisis is simultaneously at every level. But it is a crisis of prayer and apostolate. It is a crisis of people asking themselves what their lives do and could mean. Renewal still gave the priority to impersonal administration; radicalism gives it to persons.

Renewal, similarly, implied that the solution to crises was in manipulating people. Administrators were generous with education, not encouraging about new apostolates; they were interested in the reception of grants, less interested in their sisters being imprisoned for social justice. The real problem, of course, was not in directing the movements of people but in the people themselves. The approach should have been reversed. As difficult and time-consuming as it may be, religious life is improved by beginning with the aspirations and problems, the concrete vocation and potential of each member. Then there is a working

11

outwards and upwards to the community and congregation. Renewal had come from on high.

Renewal also agonized over the immediate past. It worried about fidelity to a founder. In heaven there are surely two groups of founders: one group admits with celestial honesty that he or she would have nothing to say to the problems of today out of a history centuries past; the other group comprises those geniuses who gave a lasting impetus to religious life. Yet, they are geniuses because they refuse to place their own times first; their ideas are simple, hence lasting. Clearly, it is impossible to renew a community of Christian apostles for the rigorous demands of our high-speed society and at the same time spend much time with the clothes or language of the seventeenth century. Renewal does look to the past—for mistakes, for infidelity to the present, for examples. But its only real commitment to the past is to Jesus Christ, the most rigorous and yet most creative founder.

The movement of renewal had three spatial characteristics which help to explain almost everything it attempted: it came from on high rather than from below; it took as a *sine qua non* congregational unity; it serenely expected success and urged moving slowly. Indeed, the very essence of this kind of "renewal" is that it descended from on high. This explains the emphasis on law and the non-questioning of existing structures. New superiors were elected, more democratically—but was their function different? Authority was diversified into new offices and committees —but was it really shared? More importantly was it shared with the many? There was the possibility of new life-styles and new apostolates but the road to their realization was long and sometimes bureaucratic. The point was missed that the essence of "new apostolates" is not that they are new, but that they are integral to the life of the particular people who want to be involved in them. A very strong motivation for controlled and slow-moving renewal was that it must in no way polarize or

12

divide the community and that it thereby achieve success. Just the opposite has happened; religious are increasingly polarized.

The Reversal of Renewal

Many of the present difficulties in religious life could be alleviated by reversing two of the above principles as follows. First, the decision-making process including the choice of realized vocation and education must begin with the individual. Secondly, religious life cannot be adequately adapted without the introduction of pluralism—at least during the present period of transition.

DECISION-MAKING

The past years of renewal have been, among other things, a period of demythologizing the religious life. One of the most dramatic areas of demythologizing is the entire area of "subject-superior relationships." This is part of a wider process of the secularization of authority going on throughout our society. Authority is losing its last vestiges of divine right and is being judged totally on efficacy. We no longer accept or believe that God's will can normally be identified with the superior's. Actually this always was poor theology, but it was somewhat justifiable in an illiterate peasant society. Today no young man or woman is going to submit himself or herself exclusively and totally to the direction of another human being without appeal. Our society is too filled with mobility and change, with independence and maturity for such a commitment. The obedience-command dimension narrows as education and proficiency increase. As Aristotle pointed out, we submit ourselves in societies to other people so that they will help us. Men live together for the improvement of their own lives—not for abstract order. Nor can it be argued that God has arranged religious life primarily to test men through obedience. This is a rather primitive pagan theological idea finding its unsatisfactory resolution in the book of Job. The pain of obedience comes not through obeying, but through persevering commitment. Jesus' redemptive act is not blind obedience; it is obedience to fulfill his mission.

The identification of the will of the superior with the will of God is a classic example of either bad theology or a marginal case generalized. God does not will mistakes or evil. The actions of an incompetent superior can be referred to God only in the same way that evil is permitted by God. Being a superior may give some slight claim to occasional enlightenment; it gives no reprieve from mistakes. The bishop or sister superior who "agonized" over his or her awesome responsibility for the welfare of all his or her subjects has been a widespread phenomenon in Roman Catholicism. This is, of course, ridiculous theologically and sociologically. There is no hierarchy of complete superiority and responsibility in Christianity; the hierarchy is of service. Actually, this agonizing was phony, since it rarely revealed itself in a concern for other individuals; it was often simply a method of justifying strong self-will. Nothing is easier than to claim from prayer certain knowledge of the will of God—although such an idea should be abhorrent to Christians as the heritage of Gnostics and of all fanatics.

The process of decision about community life and apostolic involvement, about finances and property disposal, about planning and reputation must be given maximum extension among all members of a community. This is their right as members— it is part of their inalienable political right. Religious life does not take away these human rights where they exist; rather it gives new ones. This demands a new look at the basic commitment of obedience. The religious enters not a family run by an individual with a twelve-year term, but commits himself to a

14

community. The commitment of religious life is primarily communal. Like the Church, the community is first. Authority exists
in a multitude of ways because every community needs authority.
This would demand the adaptation of many symbolic services so
that this commitment becomes increasingly directed towards the
entire community, both in symbol and reality. Political participation in community would be developed according to the
insights of political science and psychology. Age limits, democratic structures, elections, the methods for general critique of
institutions and finances—the gospel says nothing about these
except that Christians are to be eminently free and human and
adult. Religious life is a kind of ecclesial community, a type of
what social community could be, and so it should lead in healthy
and holy political activity. It could be the place where "new
politics" proves itself. Traditionally its politics have been either
poor, manipulated, or non-existent.

PLURALISM

The second reversal concerns unity and harmony. It is understandable that efforts should be made to preserve peace and unity
within a community with a tradition. But it is not evident that
religious can quickly discern unity from uniformity. Nothing was
more uniform than religious life, where the slightest variation in
daily schedule or dress shouted out its presence. Renewal introduced many new elements into this unchanging way of life.
Many would not, could not accept them. Careful steps were
taken to try to preserve the traditional unity and peace. But
radicalism must ask: are these real values? Certainly Christian
peace, authentic charity, and community cooperation are values.
But what is unity? peace? meaning? It is not necessary for us
to answer these important questions, for this whole process has
failed. Polarization has increased to the point where in many

15

houses it is destructive, and to where many provinces face an uncertain future. The tradition of covering up differences and problems led only to psychologically dangerous situations because the problems were no longer the rubrics of liturgy but the purpose of religious life. The very attempt to preserve unity ended in servere polarization. Polarization is an emotional and intellectual separation into two increasingly unyielding positions about *life*. Polarization is dangerous not only because it tends to be an unyielding solidification, but because it presupposes that only one side has the right to existence.

The demand for unity in renewal led to two unities—each demanding that religious life be lived in a particular way. Recent history shows that this search for constantly harmonious and monoform renewal is impossible and leads to dissatisfaction for all. The liberal direction is told it must wait for all others; the conservatives know that they are, ultimately, only living out a delaying action since the renewal movement has never retrogressed. This is unfair to both sides. *Honest pluralism must be introduced into the religious life for this time of transition.* It is as unfair to insist upon the "liberalization" of everyone as it is to hold these future-directed back from forging ahead. There has always been pluralism within the Church's religious groups; now this must extend to within the various groups. There is no merit in being able to say that no differences exist in communities; it would be a far greater witness to be able to point to diverse communities in the same area with different life-styles and ideas about worship and government who could, nevertheless, share together, live together dynamically in charity.

There are only three alternatives in a time of social change: uniform retention of the status quo, which normally implies extinction; uniform change, which often demands totalitarianism; and evolving pluralism which allows forward change and yet preserves varying degrees of tradition. As long as uniformity is insisted upon, polarization will emerge. At the same time the

16

pace of change will be frustratingly slow for the creative, for the young, for prospective joiners. It is precisely the creative and the young who may know what religious life is to be within and beyond the crisis of contemporary American life.

Pluralism is feared because it seems destructive. But pluralism is not destructive in a highly educated and individualized society. It is precisely communication between different individuals and groups which allows the mature, complex society to function well. "History shows, however, that societies which were once efficient because they were highly specialized rapidly collapsed when conditions changed. A highly specialized society is rarely adaptable. Adaptability is essential for social as well as for biological success. Therein lies the danger of the standardization and regimentation so prevalent in modern life. We must shun uniformity of environment as much as absolute conformity in behavior."[4] As the degree of uniformity in religious life decreases, the community must demand an ever greater degree of communal spirit and fiedelity to the group. When this commitment is no longer present by virtue of habit, horarium, and cloister it must come through personal commitment.

Renewal and Adaptation

We have often heard these two words—adaptation and renewal —contrasted, the message being that external adaptation is not enough and must begin with interior renewal. This can easily be an escape. If we wait until each and every Christian or religious is "interiorly perfect," we will never reach the point where externals change. This principle can be used as a block to all external change. It would deny, secondly, the sociological principle that external structures can strongly determine interior

[4] R. J. Dubos, "Man Adapting: His Limitations and Potentialities," *Environment for Man*, W. Ewald, editor (Bloomington, 1967), p. 19.

17

attitudes. Nothing shows more clearly how ineffectual this principle has been in its past application than the idea of world peace. It was long preached in Christian churches that world peace would come about if each individual were at peace within himself. The fact is that war and peace are not determined by the attitudes of insignificant citizens, but by political and social structures and a few men in control. They determine war and peace.

For the Christian communities, structures and authority figures create or preserve the atmosphere for growth and responsibility. What interior renewal can and must mean is interior conversion. This is quite a different matter. Here we are talking about a biblical *metanoia,* a deep change of mind, a radical turning to Christ. It is relatively easy to confess an appreciation for renewal and up-dating; it is far more difficult to undergo a real conversion in this area. Such a conversion would leave us open to structural criticism and unthinkable ideas. Experience shows that religious superiors with the best of intentions find it difficult to stop controlling other people, to let the responsibility for the community rest with the members rather than with bank accounts or statistics, to allow individuals to determine their own lives responsibly. This is difficult because it demands a profound psychological and spiritual conversion to values of faith. In this sense interior renewal must precede and follow external changes of structure.

The Crisis of the Times

It was theoretically possible for "renewal" to have worked. Why didn't it? Ultimately, the crisis it had to meet was too manifold and too intense; there was too much up-dating, too much renewing to accomplish from a point of departure too far back in other times and mentalities.

18

We will look again, in greater depth, at the characteristics of our time to see how they influence a style of community life and a choice of apostolates. It suffices to say that we live not in a time of crisis but in the midst of an environmental system of crises. Religious life is involved in many circles of uncertainty. There is a growing need in the world for real community, but this community is not yet clear in its dynamics; there is the possibility of renewing worship just as individual prayer becomes very difficult; there are difficult and fashionable new apostolates while formerly vast ones collapse. In short, it has become possible for provincials to claim that religious life is gone, and for novice mistresses to wonder if they know anything about it. Conversely, the novices often think they have a pretty good idea of what this life should be. All three may, in their own way, be right. Our revolutionary and changing society is a source of tension. The other source is the meaning of Jesus Christ. The new is always the honest. Jürgen Moltmann writes of the category of the "New":

If we consider our contemporary situation, we find that in all areas of life the special feature of modern times is that everywhere we are asking for something that is "new." The modern world is modern precisely because men are fascinated by the prospects of a future which so far has not taken place anywhere, and hence will be new.[5]

This is true everywhere but in the official levels of the churches. What has happened to the New of the New Testament? The radical political eschatology, considering both man's present life and the promise of his resurrection, is fearfully rejected in favor of the status quo. Moltmann points out that the dynamic future orientation of Christianity—present in the creation narrative, in the prophets, and in the coming and presence of an ambiguous Kingdom of God—cannot be removed; it lies at the heart of

[5] "The Category of the New in Christian Theology," *The Future as the Presence of Shared Hope*, M. Muckenhirn, editor (New York, 1968), p. 10.

Christianity. The theologians of hope develop Ernst Bloch's contrast between what is not yet and what is passing away. Why is man afraid of the "new," of his own future? Why does he prefer, as McLuhan puts it, to look at his culture through the rear-view mirror, and so replace creative life amidst newness with fearful wars and unbalance? Bloch has described at length the tension between what is to date unthinkable and what has actually not yet taken place.[6] The two are related. What has not happened tends to become the unthinkable and so to stop all forward movement. Yet, the human mind can always be open to the unthinkable, and so prepare for what has not yet taken place to become reality. These philosophical reflections on future change are valuable guides for any facet of Christian radical renewal.

Making the religious life new equals making it honest and making it open-ended. This not only allows—after years of taking the past for granted—but demands looking critically at every man-made institution and structure. Christianity is supposed to be the great religion which ends idolatry. Idolatry is the replacement of the Spirit and man with things. Whenever the gospel breaks through, it goes, like its master Jesus, to where religion has fashioned idols because it would not live by faith. It takes faith to exercise a charismatic critique on schools, buildings, the deployment of personnel—but it is necessary. This faith is complemented by a hope which can create new opportunities and which condemns as sinful the despairing mentality which claims that nothing but the present (that is, the past) could ever exist. Renewal was not equal to facing this burst of the Spirit into the midst of our complex world of ecclesiastical institutions, nor was it equal to solving the problems raised by the disappearence of immigrant American Catholicism and its replacement by a society run by cybernetics yet still prejudiced

---

[6] See, as an introduction to the thought of Ernst Bloch, his work *Man on His Own* (New York, 1969).

and exploitive. The present situation is not lacking in tenseness; it can seriously be suggested that many congregations and orders will not survive. Hardly anyone—prophets of doom or seers of liberation—doubt that the religious life will be quite different only ten years from now.

In the midst of this revolution we can speak of a crisis of faith. This is not surprising since all great social upheavals bring men to some kind of faith and hope. The revolution within religious life is both explained and hindered by exploring this faith-crisis. There are really two crises of faith. The first is in the difficulty present planners and administrators have in admitting the depth of the crisis in religious life. They have not yet recognized the ineffectiveness of renewal to create truly new forms, and some defend renewal and administrative procedures as strongly as they once defended punishing the novices for using their "worldly names." This crisis is the weakness and inability to have confidence in the providence of God for the future. They want God to provide, but to provide something not too surprising, something under their control and sponsorship. They are coldly afraid of the unknown future of religious life. Most of their sisters and brothers in the community experience a parallel crisis. They speak of newness and excoriate much of the past, but secretly many of them also wish for an orderly transition. Their inability is to recognize existentially and to take seriously their immersion in a revolution. The first step toward peace within these uncertainties and challenges is to recognize the time for what it is: a summons to radical change in the Church and society. As long as it is not so viewed, effort toward radical renewal is wasted and obstacles seem insuperable. Hope in a time of real revolution is only possible when the revolution and its outcome are taken seriously. Faith and hope, promise and development belong together. In the old static religious life monks and friars and sisters were not future-directed. They lived from the past in a present of gray sameness. Now their only hope is to develop colorful hope; to recognize the present for what it is—the condition of a livable future.

RADICALISM

We already begin to see, by contrast with the process of slow and limited "renewal," what the radical approach to building a better future for religious life would be. First, there must be a critique of words, of structures, of history. This critique must begin at point zero, with no presuppositions other than the most basic values of the evangelical and ecclesial community. The critique must be conducted in an atmosphere which makes such a critique psychologically possible.[7] We have already mentioned that renewal should have begun with the psychological level, enabling committees, self-studies, chapters, innumerable meetings to be more effective and less cruelly tense. Radical critique is impossible except in an atmosphere of personal honesty, and where the person practices that institutional asceticism by which he is liberated from emotional bonds to buildings and names. The Dominican theologian, Jean-Pierre Jossua, describes this as a kind of "brief of evaluation" (*cahier des charges*).[8] He sees four sections of this critique: (1) a criticism of the categories in which the religious life has been described; (2) an active critique which the contemporary perspective of secularization exercises upon the religious life; (3) a critique fashioned by the new kind of global mentality brought about by the

[7] What Rosemary Haughton says of formation and transformation can be applied to renewal and radicalism. "Formation, according to a law which is holy and just and good, is necessary if man is to live. Yet, in practice, if its influence is unbroken, it leads not to life but to death of love by asphyxiation. Transformation, therefore, can only occur when formation breaks down, and this often happens because people break the law, because they sin." *The Transformation of Man* (Springfield, 1967), p. 35.

[8] Remarks of J.-P. Jossua, O.P., "Echange sur la vie religieuse," *Christus*, 16 (1969), pp. 254ff.

problems of the third world and technological breakthroughs; (4) an outline of the scriptural and theological foundations which are the basis of religious life: following, sign, renunciation, evangelical and "worldly" values. The following pages have been written in the perspectives of secularization and social change. It would remain for another book to try to discover with the help of the critical-historical study of the New Testament the theological fundamentals for religious life in the New Testament. What Jossua means by his first critique is a questioning of the very words we use in religious life. They are loaded, at times scandalous, weak, or ambiguous. "Spiritual life," "losing a vocation," "secular," "vows," "apostolate," have all been so diluted or improperly (and idolatrously) applied that they can hardly be used in public. Unfortunately, there is an underlying value present in these poorly employed phrases, but we cannot reach it because of the scars which history has left upon our theological language in these areas. Like the philosophers of the analysis of language, we must recognize how much our actions, our vision of the future is imprisoned by our fear of creating or using new terms. (Naturally, this imprisonment is only intensified when attempts are made to "freeze" such language, to canonize it by magisterial statement or by ecclesiastical law.)

(1) *Let God Be God*   The primacy in criticism and planning as well as living belongs to God. God's will is not identifiable with man's, either with the saint's or the superior's. His plans for the Church and for his Kingdom may be different from those of a venerable Mother General or an Archbishop. His characteristics of transcendence of every structure have to be reconsidered; we cannot localize him into our projects. We must learn to discover him everywhere in his creation and his family of man.

(2) *The Religious Follows Jesus Christ*   This means that the New Testament is a *literal standard* for community life

23

and efficacy. The religious follows Christ; he or she does not re-place him in the school or foreign mission; he or she exists to point to Christ, to retire when Christ is present. The religious life, like Christ's life, is something mutable, adjustable, variable. It is so because it is poor and celibate. It has supernatural goals and is not only free of crippling commitments to a past ideal or a present system, but is bound to be critical of such things—for they may become quasi-idols as the Temple was to the Jews.

(3) *The Gospel's Radicalism* The gospel places persons first, even over religious institutions. The gospel does not allow a credibility gap between what the real Christian says and does. The gospel places complete confidence in the providence of God from day to day. The gospel loves individual people unto death and will not sacrifice them for human laws. The gospel's ultimate standard is charity, not total obedience to men. The gospel is love, and so religious life can be judged as to whether, like charity, it is "kind, patient, etc." (I Cor. 13:4ff.).

(4) *People First* The Johannine theology on charity is really another way of saying you cannot claim to put God first if you easily put people second. It is difficult enough to imagine that each local community is receiving impulses from the Pope or from its venerable founder; it is incredible to think that the immediate source of it all is God. Theologians are telling us that God and Jesus Christ are as much ahead of us as above us. So, perhaps God's greatest influence in religious life, as in the Church and in society, is in our dialectic with him in building the future. We must return again to the idea that religious life builds up from below. The individual who commits himself to the community does not thereby lose anything of his importance as a human being or a Christian. In fact, the community gains. There is no need (and it would be intolerable) to give up political and human rights to be immersed in a community when what is needed is the greatest degree of individual compe-tence and dedication. Similarly, in the apostolate the individual

24

comes first. We cannot prefer private grants, peaceful relationships with exploiting companies, for this kind of anti-Christian activity catches up (is catching up, right now) with the churches. Faith allows us to place the poor and disenfranchised first in our apostolates; charity warns we must do so. The community is placed first when people are first. "Formed," characterless religious may preserve the old forms of community life, but they destroy religious life now that it is faced with the burdens of self-justification and relevance. The kind of community which will survive is one built upon individual honesty and independence. These qualities do not destroy community but allow it to grow at the deepest level of mutual involvement. Somehow the strongest persons form the most intense communities.

(5) *Experimentation* The Roman Catholic Church was supposed, as of 1965, to enter into a period of extensive experimentation; this was the elastic principle of much of what the Council did. There was almost none! There has been much change, but little experimentation. Experimentation involves controlled development of alternatives and evaluation and it expects creativity and risk. The only way we can develop new forms of the religious life without serious dangers to that life as it is now is by experimentation. Not to experiment may be to invite rebellion or decline. There is a union today—it can be traced to people as different as Jesus Christ, Karl Marx, and John Dewey—between theory and practice.[9] Theory is developed out of practice, and research is done alongside of controlled experimentation. The value of the theoretical is not denied, but it is spared the sorry isolation which results in new ideas never changing anything. The great need for concrete improvement in human life receives sign, hope, and practical aid through the experimental union of research and action. Here theology

---

[9] See T. F. O'Meara, O.P. and D. M. Weisser, O.P., "The End of Theology?" *Projections: Shaping an American Theology for the Future* (New York, 1970).

becomes person-oriented and change-oriented. It recovers the biblical union wherein word is act or event. The prophetic word to the crisis situations of human life is made concrete in the renewal of social institutions through whatever contribution can come from Christian community life. Theology (thinking-about-being-a-Christian) finds its orientation and source in action for the future. This action is not "doing good." Nor is it an empirical and autonomous experience whether in the religious or social spheres. It is the word of God rediscovered in the form of effective secular servant. It involves being, becoming, doing, learning. Thinking is not prior or superior to, or independent of action. Thinking takes place in action; research is not only validated but inspired by program and structure. If this is becoming the general method of humanity, the approach toward life and the future, it is clear that religious life can legitimately expect to find new styles and lasting solutions through experimentation.

(6) *The Signs of the Times* Adapting secular dress is not the essence of listening to the signs of the times. The times and its signs are far too cosmic for that. It is important that religious communities be able to discern trends and challenges appearing for the Church and their own work. Communities that have people who can tell what is happening are fortunate. Training members in the social sciences and contemporary theology offers a greater possibility of not only recognizing but fashioning the future.

If all of this is unrealistic, then radicalism can be replaced by renewal. But if the worlds of the Middle Ages, industrial Europe, and World War II America are being replaced by new and complex systems, the unrealism is in those who through lack of faith or intelligence presuppose that there is no crisis— whether in the Church or in its mission.

2. Between Sin and Grace

In a time of crisis it is possible to continue to live and to grow only if the crisis is recognized. It is possible to create new ways of life only if charism and grace are given to those standing within the crisis. Charism and Christian grace, even the Holy Spirit, are conditioned by an honest recognition of the intensity and nature of the crisis. This recognition is itself grace. Man survives, relatively unprotected by nature, while other species are diminished or become extinct because of his ability to transcend the forces of changing nature with his mind. Now man faces new kinds of threats no less total. These are threats of annihilation through his own social and technological powers. War is the obvious example; but there are other subtler and no less devastating threats. Erich Fromm's book *The Revolution of Hope* is based upon their danger.

A spectre is stalking in our midst whom only a few see with clarity. It is not the old ghost of communism or fascism. It is a new spectre: a completely mechanized society, devoted to maximal material output and consumption, directed by computers; and in this social process man himself is being transformed into a part of the total machine, well fed and entertained, yet passive, unalive and with little feeling.[1]

We no longer live in a time of natural threats, since man is controlling the environment and setting his own artificial environment above nature. Crises arise from selfish, commercial,

[1] (New York, 1968), p. 1.

27

and unplanned technology dehumanizing its creators. These crises are social and human, in the sense that they are crises of how men live with each other in a world of great economic possibility and great technological power, and they are crises of life in the sense that we must think and pray in order to discover through reflection what life is. Finally, we must attain a new level of risk, courage, and asceticism to put man above machine, human values above commercial profits.

Every institution is being questioned. We need not think that the world has gone mad, or that an unthinking youth is responsible for all of this. In fact, just the opposite is true. It is *thinking* which has made us critical of our institutions; and it is our institutions' total or long-standing lack of thinking which has rendered them open to severe criticism. Since we are in the midst of a vast technological crisis, one which makes traveling to the moon and the total destruction of mankind equally real, new demands are placed upon human life. The attitudes of the 1850's or 1950's will not work before an information and population explosion. Television brings the horrors of domestic injustice and foreign wars into the home daily in color and asks why they are necessary. It is part of the crisis to think thoughts which have been said to be incapable of concrete realization. A projection of new values is also a rediscovery of the past. Jesus Christ provided a view of man. It was a radical, dangerous, impossible one; it was subsequently differentiated, compromised, practiced by an élite, etc. The present is so exciting in its honesty because, for the first time in centuries, people are asking whether the real radicalism of the Hebrew and Christian scriptures, the American Bill of Rights—all the best of man's aspirations—might not be taken seriously.

If stable institutions like government and education are going through real crises, we should not be surprised that the Church and its institutions are going through them. (Actually, we *should*

28

be surprised, since for two centuries the churches have usually been able either to escape or to combat every notion of crisis.) We are unusually blessed to be living in this time of crisis. Perhaps many religious dreamed once of how exciting it would be to create and change the community they belonged to. Now the opportunity is here, and many are afraid. The crisis in the Roman Catholic Church finds a special focus in religious life. Nowhere has more effort been spent on renewal; nowhere is dissatisfaction so apparent in terms of numbers; nowhere is there such a multitude of problems. This is to be expected. It shows perhaps that the religious communities are again the avant-garde of the Church. By highly educating their members, by engaging in differentiated apostolates, by attracting thousands of new members in the past thirty years, they have made themselves particularly capable of recognizing and being exposed to crises. Inasmuch as religious persons stand at the point where contemporary American society meets the new revolutions, they encounter both the secular revolution and the kerygma of the Church. Also, the religious have a tradition of responding to crisis situations. This does not mean that they inevitably renew themselves and live. Often enough in the history of the Church, religious communities (and in times far less crucial than the 1970's in America) did not renew—either not at all, or not radically—and died out. Their last trace is being removed as their founders are taken from the liturgical calendar. New response in Christian communities came sometimes through renewal but more often through *new forms* of religious life. The response to the crisis was a new kind of religious life: scandalous, non-establishment, intellectually open, shockingly mobile for the times. For instance, the first friars (thirteenth century) combined mobility, education, poverty, and democracy.

29

THE NATURE OF THE CONTEMPORARY CRISIS

It is possible that Marshall McLuhan and many others are wrong. It is possible that our present crises are insignificant, that things will return to a status quo similar to the past. This book is based upon the opposite point of view. The essential aspect of the contemporary crisis for anyone who wishes to survive it creatively is to understand it as radically serious and historically rare. It is radically serious because it permeates so many dimensions of our life. The protests within the universities are not unrelated to those in monastic religious orders or at political conventions. Whether you are speaking to advertising agents, philosophy teachers, or marriage counselors you inevitably encounter the new tendency in group processes and personal relationships. From so many points of view the aware observer is forced to conclude that American society is divided over the choice between process and content, between thinking and facts, between creativity and preservation. Each of these dilemmas is only a different way of expressing the same problem.

Many people—in worlds as disparate as that of the film critics and the university presidents—are carrying forward the idea born almost a hundred years ago: that Western culture is at the end of something. The first fifty to seventy years of this idea had a rather dour history since they did not convey its correlate: that we are also at the beginning of something important. Nietzsche's announcement that "God is dead" was really the proclamation of the end of nineteenth-century European Christendom; he called for a "devaluation" of all ordinary values. (Those who observe the weakening and breakdown of our once hallowed political structures—state legislatures, party conventions, etc.—are no longer so shocked by the call to reverse values.) Kierkegaard saw the first two millenniums of Christianity as simply a prelude whose task was to show Christendom as

30

bankrupt in terms of close worldly unions between church and the establishment. Heidegger affirmed Nietzsche's insight, saying that the fundamental reflection of Western man had gotten off the track in both philosophy and faith; it rejected mystery, and was too content with clear-cut explanations about reality. For him history had destroyed fundamental thinking. Religious leaders have remarked that with its two world wars Europe seemed to slip under a cloud or a curse. Now, even in the "new world," Marshall McLuhan says that we are at as radical a change in cultural history as when man transcended the village at the beginning of the bronze age.

Parallel to this is promise for the future. Our hope is the sudden awareness, hardly a decade old, that it is possible and even primary to allow our new technological abilities in automation, travel, and communications to make our world wealthier but more human. Institutes to study the future show how we can trace future alternatives and warn ourselves against some of them. The new student left calls for a return to the basic American principles of liberty and justice for all. We are, in short, at the beginning of a unique era where we can fashion our future. Yet we do not really believe this. We hold onto the belief that primitive powers determine the coming times; otherwise we would not continue to act so irresponsibly politically, economically, and ecclesially.

If it is true that we are at a crossroads in human history, we will need new forms of Christian dedication. Even if the present crisis is greater in magnitude that than the collapse of the Roman Empire or the Renaissance-Reformation, there is no reason to be ultimately dismayed. *It is awareness of this crisis which holds the key to overcoming the disastrous possibilities of polarized religious life, and which unlocks the future of promise.* As long as we cling to the hope that a radical crisis is not at hand, we will be content merely to revise past structures. We will review our immediate past instead of mining the riches of a New

31

Testament past and a technological future. We will belong to that great group which is confident, since they know the 1950's so well, that nothing truly revolutionary could happen. *What is necessary for belief in the religious life is belief in crisis, and in the power of the Spirit and the future of man to transcend it creatively.*

Crisis stands between past and future. The gospel of John uses the Greek word *krisis* to signify the new kind of moment which has broken in with Jesus Christ, broken into the world of men and religions. Jesus is the definitive word, the incarnate Word of God's grace and promise to man. All men must explicitly or implicitly encounter that word and decide for or against the Word of God for them. The moment deciding encounter is the Johannine *krisis*.

> The concepts light, truth, life, and freedom explain each other: so do the concepts darkness, falsehood, death, and bondage . . . [they] denote the double possibility of human existence: to exist either from God or from man. They all imply that only in the knowledge of his creaturehood can man achieve true understanding of himself; this is the *light* that illumines his way. Only in such knowledge does he perceive the truth—the true reality which makes itself available to him in the revelation of God. . . . Each man is, or once was, confronted with deciding for or against God: and he is confronted anew with this decision by the revelation of God in Jesus.[2]

A crisis whether it is universal and secular or personal and religious involves an encounter and a decision. It involves the past and the future. On the religious horizon it stands between sin and grace. Here we adopt Heidegger's use of the word *destruction,* as when he speaks about the decline of open thinking within the prison of declining scholasticism. This destruction is not something the critic or philosopher or politician

---

[2] Rudolf Bultmann, "The Theology of the Gospel of John and the Johannine Epistles," *Theology of the New Testament,* II (New York, 1958), p. 21.

causes. Hitler and Stalin, Martin Luther King and Gandhi are not the central figures in such destruction; they are the victims or heroes in larger dramas. This destruction is brought by history itself. History and the mysterious élan of human life and progressive evolution witness with approval the collapse of institutions which in their permanence would impede man. Such a destruction is often a conflict in which the innocent are martyred and the evil temporarily triumphant. History shows itself as a series of rises and falls, and societies which would survive must try to read the signs of destruction and renaissance.

Excessive fidelity to the past at the risk of stopping or maiming the present can eventually lead to violent destruction. When a group chooses to fight against (or even simply to watch from the sidelines) the tide of history, it invites unwanted and often ruthless destruction. Religious institutions have been notoriously slow to perceive the signs of the times. In spite of their lasting relationship to the Holy Spirit (whose divinity they insult and render incredible by their obtuseness), they tend in time of crisis to retreat and to opt for survival at any cost. One blessing of secularization is that religious institutions themselves must be judged not only by the Spirit at work in unseen grace, but by the same Spirit at work in the world of men. The relationship between sin and clinging to the past would be a fruitful one for exploration. Certainly, much could be gleaned from studying Jesus' attitudes toward the ossification of the Jewish religion of his time. His attitude toward the union of religion and the past was frequently severe. His own preaching emphasized both the present and the future far more than the past. Jürgen Moltmann's writings on the resurrection have shown how Jesus' own life, *including* his resurrection, was future oriented—toward our future and his future.[3] His resurrection,

[3] See Jürgen Moltmann, *Theology of Hope* (New York, 1967); "The Future as Threat and Opportunity," *The Religious Situation—1969* (Boston, 1969), pp. 921ff.; *Religion, Revolution and the Future* (New York, 1969);

that point in space and time in which the eschatological and historical join, has itself a future. It is no surprise that Jesus was eminently critical of the identification of the worship of God with the unchanging. While he showed great concern for the sacramental, the use of the material as a sign of holy presence, he also initiated the process of religious secularization by giving primacy to interior religion and by his disclosure of the Trinity —a God of action and differentiation. Belief in the Holy Spirit is a constant warning against centering religion in the past, for the "functional personality" of the Spirit is found in our world only in terms of the present and future.

CONFESSION OF SIN

For the Christian the past can be a source of sin. When man clings only to the past, he lacks faith and may bring forth destruction. What this means to the present debate and activity over changing religious life is that confession of sin, an admission of sinfulness in the past, cannot be omitted. Almost every religious group has omitted it. When renewal began, things seemed to be going fairly well for religious life. It never occurred to the people involved that re-examination should begin with an honest and public critique of the past. As the tempo of change became more rapid after the Council, and as problems multiplied rather than subsided, this profoundly religious tendency—to see the difficulties of the present as partially the fruit of past abuses—rarely appeared. Certainly, recognition came increasingly to many sisters and priests who had been frustrated or injured by the past. But the "establishment" of religious orders and congregations was not in the mood for admitting the

M. Marty, editor, *New Theology* #5 (New York, 1967). W. M. Cunningham, O.P., "The Theology of Hope: An English-Language Bibliography," *Canadian Journal of Theology,* 15 (1969), pp. 131–137.

evils of the past, since many of them were convinced that what was now happening was an evil. Consequently they looked upon the past as paradise lost.

An ambiguous and inauthentic leadership only tolerates or slightly promotes renewal; it publicly admits the necessity of change, and yet sees change in direct continuity with all of the past history of the particular congregation. It seemed as if this attitude might work; the congregation would continue in blissful continuity and respectability, building one era upon another. But rising numbers of departures and increased polarization indicate that renewal led not to faith, hope, and charity but to discouragement and doubt. This itself is a sign that it was built upon shifting ground. The past was not entirely to be renewed. Part of it had to be excoriated and condemned. As long as this was not done, the community, lacking a necessary exorcism, was not free to respond to the Spirit.

As long as religious life in any of the past decades is looked upon as the ideal, radical openness to the needs of the times cannot take place. When religious life in the 1920's or the 1950's is glamorized as a time of observance and zeal, the situation becomes so confused that discussion, much less disagreement, is impossible. You cannot disagree with a saint! *One of the reasons society and the Church are changing so much is that they need to change a great deal.* The drive to critical renewal is a good thing, and it comes violently when the old structures have failed extensively and are open to mass rejection. A condition, then, of meeting the present-as-crisis is a confession of the sins of the past. It is not an admission that the past was sin, or even that the past was useless. Actually, understood within their own sphere of culture and faith, the immediately preceding decades in America are part of one of the greatest periods in the history of religious life. History is not a kind and understanding mother, but rather a stern guide urging us to go faster and more efficiently for our own good. It cannot be otherwise, for there is no newness· without an awareness of the past, distinguishing what must be retained as fruitful and treasurable from what must be discarded as erosive and moribund. Not to discern is itself sinful, not to recognize evil is the greatest sin— for it either admits a connaturality with sin so great that sin is not perceived, or it affirms that there is no such thing as sin. Never to confess sin is tantamount to denying its existence. Paradoxically religious are quite capable of denying evil in their very posed attempts to fight it.

The Sins of the Past

Each religious group must confess its own sins. It must see sin not as any past or historical form, but as infidelity to the revolutionary religious spirit of the gospel. Sin is also infidelity to the insights of the founders, although this possibility diminishes as we approach more recent centuries in which religious life was influenced by leaders with more detailed ideas and less genius. In general, the sins of religious life are frequently sins against the general spirit of the religious message of the New Testament. They place religious things and structures before religious spirit; they idolatrously tie the sovereign and mysterious will of God and the action of his Spirit to things or man-made laws, or to the fallible (or unintelligent) minds of superiors. These sin like the Pharisees, who are simply archetypes of what often befalls religion: specialization in hypocrisy and magic. They cloak ineffectiveness and superstition with righteousness and privilege. Let us consider some more common vices, the most repeated arch-sins.

(1) In the past a so-called "moral person" (the order or community) was placed above the individuals which formed it. The congregation became an end in itself: its institutions, its buildings, its finances, its "good" reputation. This denied the

36

New Testament revolution which made religion the liberator and enabler of man. Religious community exists for those entering it, not for the abstract or external glory of a name. The moral person, the larger congregation or province, survived at the expense of its members. Without consultation, they might be moved; without education, they might be placed in an unexpected situation. For the sake of a unity and harmony they were deprived of voice in planning for the future by those who knew better. Individuals were unjustly sacrificed or crushed for what are ultimately materialistic ends, for the survival of institutions is primarily a materialistic and not a religious goal. Others had their reputation or future reversed in order to preserve the status quo. Where these things existed or exist, they must be confessed. The evil of the past—however extensive it was or was not—must be renounced, and conversion to a new era of justice be stated.

(2) One aspect of institutional primacy is the misuse of individuals. Preparation is part of every ministry. Vocation and preference are also ways in which the Spirit draws people to preach the Kingdom. Mistreating Christian apostles as pawns to be moved by a "Superior" on the board is unjust. Contrary to much of the spiritual writings of second-rate writers, acceptance of some personal destiny contrary to the deepest history and horizons of individual personality, while it is indeed a request which may be made by God, is, like all things heroic, rather rare. The idea of having a community of fifty or five hundred religious all involved in heroic acts of obedience and apostolates contrary to their personal exigencies is ridiculous. Similarly grotesque is the frequent use of the call to heroic virtue simply to cover up ineptitude or total lack of province-wide planning.

(3) One of the greatest vices is the very process (unperceived by its victims) which has led to the large number of relatively unemployable religious. They are often among the

most reactionary, and rightly so, for they see the totality of their world snatched away from them. *They really perceive the extent of the past's formation upon them and the difficulty of their embracing any alternative.* Their problems are not dogmatic nor are they emotional in the normal sense. They are rooted in a formation process which accomplished the exact reverse of education: it left them helpless before change. They have been totally shaped into one system. This system had as its poles a single faith-thought system (textbook Thomism), a certain law (Constitutions and the Code of Canon Law), a reassuring central directive, a boring but ultimately rewarding (in the sense of eschatological merit) end, and a gnostic (setting aside a privileged group) liturgy and spirituality. Now they are "destroyed" by the changes in education and the Church. Few programs have arisen to help these many religious. The creation of a process which would begin with emotional fears and end with courage joined to real competence is one of the most pressing needs in the Catholic Church. Otherwise vocational incompetency will pose an enormous burden: financial, vocational, and communal.

(4) There was a frequent hypocrisy in the past, and that was the untruthful idealization (in many senses) of biblical and traditional virtues. The novices were given the impression that the courage of a Francis Xavier and the literal following of Jesus Christ were omnipresent. One of the most painful aspects of religious life was the gap between the life as it "should" be lived (as it was preached during yearly retreats, lived in novitiates, etc.) and the way the life was actually lived in most places. The growth of the young religious seemed to involve inevitably and painfully a certain "becoming realistic," for it became all too clear that the religious community did not exist as it was described in the novitiate. Thomas Aquinas' creativity may have been so creative in the thirteenth century that he was condemned by bishops twice, but such creativity was not encouraged among his followers. Certainly, one of the great blessings about the present

situation is that religious life is becoming *increasingly honest and increasingly evangelical at the same time.* It is no longer necessary to make pretenses about the gap between a monastic novitiate and a California apostolate. And at the same time, from Selma to film festivals, we do find sisters and priests in the forefront of the "action" in America.

There was a deeper hypocrisy—though one surely not true of all communities. In the midst of the present difficult times it appears that the "establishment" was not really very anxious for the zeal of Francis or Ignatius to reappear. They knew too well that this might cause great difficulty with financial supporters. It would also make them feel inferior. The status quo was psychologically necessary to them. Secondly, it came as a surprise to many that their own community could be a significant voice in the midst of the new theology or the new politics. All of this was an unwelcome and unsettling storm for a previously peaceful way of life. Past religious life had its own secular dimension; it isolated its life and ministry into safe compartments which took a certain amount of time and which involved a measured degree of effort and difference. "Imprudent" involvement in public witness, and a zeal which could end a man in prison rather than at the mayor's garden party, hardly recalled the pious virtues of statuesque Vincent de Paul or that untroublesome little black man Martin de Porres. Martin Luther King was not an Oblate or a Franciscan, and the relationships of Father Philip Berrigan and Father Daniel Berrigan to their communities have been ambiguous. The question remains: did the religious communities *really want* to be Christian apostolic-communal communities in a radical way—in literal terms of the gospel and their own traditions?

(5) One experience of religious poverty is that it scrupulously and exaggeratedly pursued the individual religious to empty himself of all monies under a quarter. Actually, the good of the Catholic Church (and perhaps of America) would have been

39

equally served if another aspect were emphasized. Our present problem is not that we have a large group of monastic profligates, but that the 1950's seem to have poured forth ugly, impractical, unwieldy, gigantic, and now empty buildings. These expensive buildings are signs of sin. The sin is not complicated; it involved individual self-will and absence of consultation. Often the "edifice complex" was a psychological problem representing the superior's revenge upon the hard times of his childhood.

Money is power. A critical glance must be given to the problem of finances. Money can exercise enormous control, even over religious. It controls their education (which is crucial for apostolic effectiveness) and it controls their future (a source of anxiety and fear). We will see later that the vow of poverty has nothing to do with financial control; it is basically an eschatological witness to the world and a commitment to communal life. Community finances are not a religious matter at all; they have a relation to poverty only when the community is injured in its life and work, or when they cause scandal. Both of these negative effects of finances seem to come more frequently from the administrators of finance rather than from the individual members. As the individual religious becomes more mature he should expect that the money he earns will be used well. His concern for the apt dedication of his earnings to the advancement of the Kingdom is part of his commitment to evangelical poverty, and it cannot be alienated from it. Poverty does not eliminate responsibility. Just as evangelical poverty would demand that an individual leave a community where the cumulation of wealth had become central, so it would demand that he leave a community where money was grossly mismanaged. Both are radically wasteful. Obviously the connection of finances with secrecy and control must end. The widest possible consultation on the use and misuse of personnel and property is essential for avoiding the sins to which cumulative (and secret) finances led in the past.

GRACE AS AN HORIZON OF OUR WORLD

During a time of crisis the past manifests itself as partly sin, the future as grace. There are many ways of conceiving Christian grace. All of them must be kept in mind. When any one is over-emphasized at the expense of the other dimensions, we soon find ourselves in schisms or devotional aberrations. Grace is a gift of God; but, it involves man's response. It allows man to be fully man by transcending himself in belief and love, but it does this without unusual effects and is most dynamic when it enters into the marrow of human life, rather than when it pretends to the extraordinary. Grace is the milieu of human life and finds its greatest intensity in the Christian message and impulse to love. Yet grace is not only horizon, or God's attitude toward mankind, or something within me—it is also an impulse from God to help me remain faithful to him, creative of my true self, and responsive to my neighbor. Grace allows me to balance my Christian role in this life with my beginning of the eschatological Kingdom of God right now.

Grace has always been viewed as something dynamic, and it is not so much a theological error as immaturity to conceive of it solely as a state. Even this state, this being in the new creation, is viewed within the Bible in terms of personal life and the unfolding of history. Grace is always active, whether we mean the impulse by which we respond to God's many invitations or the confession of our faith that we hope to be now and in the future part of the People of God. The theology of Aquinas which saw grace as the beginning of the eschaton ("the seed of glory") was correct; it opens the future within an historical and eschatological continuity. Today's theologians of hope claim that Christianity is eschatology. They point out that Jesus' resurrection also means our rising from the dead, that salvation history

41

is open-ended, full of expectation of the new. We must go beyond another simplistic view of the Christian message about the future—the view that centers upon an apocalyptic end. What kind of end is coming remains a mystery. Far more of Christian eschatology is concerned with the continuity between what has been begun in Jesus and his second coming.

The rediscovery of the historical is characteristic of modern man. For him what is historical is real. Western man sees the future increasingly within his grasp, waiting to be built. For the contemporary American change is the *pattern* of life. Salvation history, process theology, the theology of the new and of creative hope are the manifestations of this deep thought-form in the Christian consciousness. This helps to explain the rediscovery of grace as dynamic milieu and impulse. Faith is a response and a perspective on life born of the cross/resurrection of Jesus Christ and of his second coming into redeemed secularity and history. Hope bridges faith and love/service and is the power of creating the future under the Spirit. These recollections of the process of life and theology simply illustrate today's shift from status to function, from ontological sign to effective, credible sign. Neither prayer nor contemplation is set aside, but they are verified in action.

Does Religious Life Have a Future?

But is there any hope, any hope for religious life? It is said of the East Germans that they "vote with their feet." Are the many people who are leaving the religious life, even the priesthood and the episcopacy, voting with their feet? Paradoxically, while thousands of religious can leave their profession in one year, we do not see (and this is rare in history) a parallel, significant decline in church membership nor a lack of interest in religion. The fact is that there has not been in centuries such a concern with the religious dimension. Are religious, then, entrapped in an impossible situation, part of history's inescapable destructive process? Does the religious life have a future?

St. Paul in Romans casually defines Christians as those who have hope (Rom. 8:18). We have seen that hope no longer entails a dreamy imagining of utopia, but a risking to build the future. It is no longer a static belief in the future, but a power to fashion and to believe in what we dare to believe lies both in our hands and in God's: the Kingdom of God, in the midst of us and coming to us out of the future. Previously in the religious life hope was reduced to a static expectation of a future life different from this life. Hope was emasculated and thus open to the attacks of many who, like Karl Marx, accused Christian eschatology of canonizing present misery and stopping progress. The "non-worldliness" of religious life was mistakenly used to frustrate creativity, to calm authentic fears about irrelevance and personal uselessness, to implement unjust and hasty decisions.

This question about the future demands not only hope but realism. Thousands have asked this question. Or has it been asked for them? Wouldn't many religious say that they had not really posed the question, but in the back of their minds the question came to consciousness? The question is important, but we should avoid panic. After all, we have only been renewing the institutions of the Roman Catholic Church, institutions little changed from 1000 to 200 years, for four to six years. The number of priests and sisters who have left is really not large, if the crisis is as great as it may be. The pressures of life in the United States today are tremendous—loneliness, threat, disintegrating institutions (educational, political, military). These tremendous pressures the religious must also survive, and added are the changes in religious life, in apostolates, in the Church. It is not surprising that we are still peeling off the layers of problems.

There are reasons for saying there is no future. We do not

43

know what the future is. Why commit yourself totally for life when no one knows what's going to happen? On the other hand, you may feel that you know what the future will be like— but that it's hard to put into words. Or one can feel that this isn't *my* future. I entered something else and that no longer exists. If what I vowed myself to has changed until I barely recognize it, shouldn't I leave? How can I be committed to both forms when they are so different? What about all the very talented people who are leaving? Aren't they the best judges?

This litany is depressing, but it can be a lesson in the new Christian hope—which is realistic and critical, as well as optimistic. We are asking whether there is any hope for religious life. This question cannot be answered apart from a personal dimension. The answer will not be a brilliant theory which ends all doubts. It can only be a catalyst for a deeper personal response born of an individual's experience. There is a future for the religious life, but it is based in an unusual way upon the individual's own perspective. A man or woman who wishes to enter or to remain in this life of communal Christian apostolate must agree on three things (I think there are people who do agree on these, as well as young people who will want this when it is presented clearly and lived out before them): (1) The admission that we live in a time of transition, rapid change, and real crisis. (2) A commitment to the living and preaching (in the widest sense) of the truly basic values in the events and message of the New Testament, even to the point of loneliness, uncertainty, persecution, risk, isolation, and death. (3) Acceptance of the fact that these two poles will have to be brought together in the individual's life in community *creativity* and *ambiguity*. Let us look at each.

(1) Crisis in the world has been discussed a great deal. It is important to develop a *psychological* awareness of crisis. As long as we think that Church, world, and community will calm down and return to a time in which answers are either there or given

44

to us, to a time when we do not have to be learning, updating, changing, we nourish a mentality which is suicidal and unhappy. Each person, no matter how radical or creative, has traces of this attitude. At some level our psyches still long for the status quo; otherwise we would not be so upset when we run into contradictions. We would be able to see the over-all situation more calmly, not surrendering either new or old values. We must initiate ourselves into a mental world-view which will allow us to survive through crisis. We must concern ourselves with tactics instead of goals. If we are fixed on goals, on wanting big changes too fast, we are looking for a status quo, a new one, but, nevertheless, a static situation. And yet, we are told, everything will change, and change rapidly, except change. This is really the old approach. This is standing still and having our future changed by others. We should be asking, "How can I initiate change?"

(2) How often we have heard of the values of the New Testament, but how we have watered them down! We say God so loves the world that he becomes a man—then we manipulate hundreds of people and shun the poor. Real evangelical values drive people into prison and generally turn things upside down. If *we* do not take the values of Jesus Christ seriously, there is no future for religious life. That is not a shock statement—it is based upon the recognition that one world is emerging with the incarnation of the sacred in the secular. The Christian appears not from heaven or within churches—he comes out of life, invention, and politics. The narrowing of credibility gaps parallels the shift from two worlds to one world of incarnation. Religious cannot claim to follow the gospel and then neglect the Sermon on the Mount.[4]

(3) We need "creative ambiguity" to remain between the above two poles and to try to unite them. This again is a

---

[4] Thomas Aquinas writes: "Our Lord's Sermon on the Mount contains the complete sum of information on the Christian life." *Summa Theologiae,* I–II, q. 108, a. 3.

psychological attitude like the first. Can I survive psychologically in a life where I have to help in fashioning that very way of life? Not everyone can do this. Can I do this with the added pressure of celibate life? Can I be open to new dimensions, to risk, to change? Can I live in this ambiguity? This does not mean I have to live in it alone. Here we return to deep faith, to others around me, to community. So I must ask if I find community. Are there signs that my communities are moving toward this, for this is necessary as a support in this situation. Creative ambiguity does not mean standing alone as a unique person but implies community in this situation.

Our answer is not derived from prophecy, but from taking currents we can point to now and extending them into the future. We have to rediscover the past, but discover it in its ambiguity so it can give us courage in a present moving into the future. This is the difference between dynamic Christian hope and static religiosity. Years before the conquest of the moon Teilhard de Chardin wrote: "The whole future of the Earth, as of religion, seems to me to depend on awakening our faith in the future."

3. Calling and Commitment

THERE are Christians who through their choice and on-going profession of a communal apostolate at a level of intensity witness and proclaim the following of the gospel. Ordinary parlance refers to them as sisters, brothers, Benedictines or Franciscans. The technical (and mainly legal) designation has been *religious*. There has never been any claim that these men and women alone were truly religious. And in conversations of an ecumenical nature the term appears ridiculous. We no longer, furthermore, see the People of God as an army made up of clearly separate groups. The layman reads the Scriptures; the sister distributes communion; the salesman presides over the parish council. We have a spectrum of different functions and life-styles, a spectrum in which it is not easy to distinguish where precisely one life-style begins and another ends. It is not so easy to understand how a Catholic husband who is a teacher radically differs from a Christian teaching brother, and so forth. There are many kinds and levels of apostolic Christians in the Church, and it is obvious that laymen and sisters and seminarians tend to give more leadership in the frontline of the Church than do pastors. *States* of life have been turned upside down as we begin to designate *and* evaluate by function. Orders and vows no longer constitute a lasting status as much as they ordain to a function which implies a life-style. Thomas Aquinas pointed this out long ago when he called attention to the fact that ordination is diversified because it is aimed at function.[1] Even more important is the picture given by the New Testament of a pluralistic early Christian community with a functional leadership.[2] The choice in the first century of secular, action-centered words for Christian ministry—overseer, counselor (presbyter), preacher, teacher, announcer—illustrates a radical shift in the idea of religion and priesthood, an innovation obscured by the establishment in the Middle Ages of social and religious structure in long-term states.

When at all possible, the following pages will describe "religious" through other terms, for instance, "communal apostles." This implies neither exclusiveness nor privilege. It involves, rather, professional and full-time commitment (involving other aspects such as sign-value and crisis-involvement) to the Christian apostolate, publicly and lastingly professed within a community of communities. Edward Schillebeeckx can say that celibacy is the essence of religious life, because celibacy is the sign and entrance to a level of community and apostolate. There are many levels of Christian community; religious life is oriented to a degree of involvement and full-time occupation, an involvement which builds upon a certain kind of family, the celibate community. This community allows for certain forms of challenging apostolates, apostolates realistically possible only for members of such a family and community.

Men and women who choose this way of life are primarily called to take a special part in the world-wide work of Christ. In this sense their "vocation," their calling, is their existence, for here calling is mission and life. Jesus sent his apostles and disciples and their converts to preach the Good News to all men. As God's Word incarnate in a particular time and place,

---

[1] *Summa Theologiae*, III q. 37, a. 1, ad. 1.

[2] John L. McKenzie, *Authority in the Church* (New York, 1966; Hans Kung, *The Church* (New York, 1968); G. Dix, "The Ministry in the Early Church," *Apostolic Ministry* (London, 1957); E. Schweizer, *Church Order in the New Testament* (Naperville, 1961).

Jesus could only preach to certain people alive then. Similarly, all subsequent Christian apostles are sent to and limited by the people alive in their time. All potential "Hearers of the Word" live in a specific age. The world and the people in it affect Christ's on-going mission deeply. *This book contains reflections upon how prominent and emerging factors in contemporary American society explain the crisis within religious life and call for radical responses. Those factors are: American secularization; social change; the cybernetic, sociotechnical,*[3] *and electronic revolutions; and a new kind of person and a corresponding need for community.*

If the Christian mission is to people alive now—born into, growing and developing within our culture—how they think, live, judge, work, recreate, and pray is of the utmost importance. Like the New Testament with its different books, the apostolate is not one eternal methodology, but is determined by the culture to which it wishes to speak. Future religious will be increasingly men and women of their own cultures. If religious life is to exist in coming generations, it must appear to the young generations of the nations of the world as something challenging, something worthwhile and intelligible, something alive. It must also appear as something variable, flexible, pluralistic. In our age of rapid change many estimate a generation to be only seven years. While the world grows smaller through the development of the mass-media and economic cooperation, generations grow apart and new cultures forge their differences. Vatican II's *Pastoral Constitution on the Church in the Modern World,* singles out four explosions: the knowledge explosion, the population explosion, the problem of the cities, the problem of international communications. Others talk of the explosion

---

[3] "Sociotechnical" refers to the influence of new technological systems on human environment; the word comes from Herbert Richardson, *Toward an American Theology* (New York, 1957). See also *Projections: Shaping an American Theology for the Future* (New York, 1970), and Erich Fromm, *The Revolution of Hope* (New York, 1968).

of mass-media and automation; the explosion of periodicals, books, and schools; the explosion of space-exploration, and control through medicine or weapons of destruction.

THE NEED FOR A PHENOMENOLOGY OF CONTEMPORARY AMERICA

It is not possible to undertake here such a vast task as a phenomenological study of America today. Let us merely indicate how important is all information which would have to bear on this topic. Since Christians live within a certain culture, the Christian churches can rediscover their original "secularity," in which they lived within a single world consecrating it to a transcendent and incarnate (and executed) God. Monasteries and convents can discover that they must again become the open centers they inevitably were at their inception. A study of the Benedictines of Europe, the Dominicans at the time of the emergence of the European university, or the Jesuits of the post-Tridentine period show how deformed has been our vision of isolation and seclusion as essential and protective of religious life. It is precisely the open community which, historically and theologically, can try to achieve its vocation. To be open means to be open to a particular time and a particular place; there is no such thing as "general" openness, for this can become dilettantism. Necessary reflection on a particular society would concern itself with how characteristics like the following influence Christians and Christian apostles.

(1) *Democracy and Participation in Government* It is taken for granted that a contemporary society is in some way democratic. The informed freedom of the citizens governs according to a majority consent. More significant is today's questioning of whether the governmental institutions (of France, the United States, South America, etc.) are adequate for providing

true representation. There is a call for greater participation and imagination. Tens of thousands of students have sacrificed months or years to join the Peace Corps, Vista, to campaign in the election of 1968, to march (some even to be killed) in the southern states. The men and women involved in these movements go beyond capitalism or pure protest; they expect their dedication, their heroic and informed action to influence governmental decision.

(2) *Changing Language and Mental Patterns* Language philosophy questions how we use words. It wants more precision in our usage of words particularly when we speak of what is non-empirical—of Spirit, grace, God, etc. Linguistic analysis is related to the need we mentioned previously: the need to ask whether the very words and categories in which we find religious life described should not be opened to new realities, should not be criticized so that they are no longer prisons. Hermeneutic, the process of interpretation and the relationship of the believer or reader to words, continues this process. How do certain texts determine me when I read them, or when I find imperatives there? How am I influenced and influential through words and my interpretations of them? Marshall McLuhan's work on the influence of media and electronic technology on our persons and life-styles carries this further. Although we do not know precisely how a changing world influences the mind, we do know that the way people think can change. The American—who lives in a country where jet travel has made railroads obsolete and where states are the size of countries elsewhere—does not have the same attitude toward space and time as people in many other parts of the world. Television changes peoples' orientation towards sound and picture, and toward reports of racism and war. The New Testament records the incarnation, God's definitive revealing Word, in terms of images and words; the Church celebrates it in liturgical signs. And so, the problem of communication is central to the Christian communal aposto-

51

late. Since grace will not change nature but only bring it to fullness, it is imperative to understand how people think and to use the media of communications to which they listen.

(3) *The New Generation and the Movement Toward the Future* Americans talk about the "generation gap." Religion is where you find it, and it is not strange that today when authentic religious experience is so noticeably absent from familiar places, it should be popping up in new and off-beat ones. Voices of prophets and mystics are heard. "Today nightclub entertainers *are* preachers, protest is ritual, and folk singers *are* prophets and theologians for the new generation. Speed kills and so does the Establishment. The young question their relationship to the structures of established society. Some reject it, some withdraw, others seek to change it. All feel more or less alienated; they are disturbed by the status quo, bogged down under pharisaical, bourgeois baggage. And in reacting, they have started what amounts to their own spiritual revolution."[4]

One has only to talk with students and young adults to see credibility gaps. The young are reacting against what seems to them to be the overly materialistic and somewhat blind (or selfish) life-style of their parents. This reaction may seem to lack sympathy for the accomplishments of this nation of immigrants; nevertheless, many young people today tend to look for involvement instead of security, creativity instead of imitation, dedication to high goals instead of enjoyment of the status quo, and respect for the individual person instead of the maintenance of a system. They refuse to accept the old defenses of ideologies and institutions, and they reject grandiose claims which are not proved by action. All of these attributes should appeal to Christians and most of them are evangelical. In many countries, in fields as diverse as theology and management planning, there is

[4] C. Hubbard, "Missing the Yellow Submarine," *Commonweal*, 89 (1968), p. 434.

what J. B. Metz calls "a categorical pre-eminence of the future."[5] The whole of modern criticism or indifference toward religion centers on the churches' indifference to the present power of man to improve his future, to the debilitation of the strongly eschatological message of the Christian gospel by fearful and ungifted ecclesiastics. One of the great challenges of contemporary theology is to understand how building a better human world is deeply related to the positive resolution of history and the second coming of Jesus Christ.

(4) *Education* Americans take education for granted. Close to half of all young Americans are attending universities. Earning power is seen as a correlate of past and on-going education. But going to school for twelve to twenty years is only one aspect of the educational situation. Education must also be *remedial* for the ghettos, *supplementary* for the handicapped, *continuing* for professional people. Economic growth, voice in government, and human maturity are seen as intimately involved in all forms of education. There is a great upsurge of interest in theological education as evidenced by the thousands of adults studying for advanced degrees in theology. There is the need to reconsider religious educational methods and systems to meet the generation gap caused by Vatican II.

Education is not the handing on of static truths, the transmitting of facts. It is a quest, a search, a disclosure, and its object is truth—truth, which takes many shapes and directions. Education is therefore a cause of change and revolution and includes the need for revolution. Some claim that the present revolution in education is actually caused by a revolution in technology, especially in electronics. Television, computers, and other forms of media have changed and are changing people's minds. Critics point out that movies are increasingly new environments and new experiences rather than primarily entertainment.

We obviously live in a world in which many new kinds of

[5] *Theology of the World* (New York, 1968), p. 148.

"language" exist. This makes it increasingly difficult for the Word of the gospel to be heard and to be understood. Almost everything that is happening today—from linguistic analysis to systems which support life on the moon—is concerned with new uses and new sets of symbols.

(5) *The Problems of One World* America shares in the common problems of the world. Conversely, the world's attention is focused on the fact that in this land of affluence millions are relatively poor, that our racial problems demand solution or they will lead to disaster. The problems of international disarmament and peace, of fair economic growth for all levels of society are equally important. In short, the world seems to have three great problems: peace, poverty, justice. The world's problems are the Church's problems. The Church's message is not identical, of course, with a solution to social unrest. Yet, the message of the Incarnation affirms the radical dignity of every man and woman. In view of the Parousia, it hopefully proclaims a progressive fulfillment in the world's social and cultural affairs. While going beyond the problems of social change, the Church cannot be aloof or "transcendent" any more than Jesus Christ could be aloof and yet be a man with compassion for those who hunger and thirst.

(6) *Secularism* The American cities seem to be the epitome of secularity. Phenomenologically, the Church does not loom large on their horizon as it does in Florence or Cologne. Yet American cities contain the largest percentage of practicing urban Catholics in the world. The process of secularization is not necessarily inimical to the Christian message. Many theologians see the Old and New Testaments as the impetus for secularization.[6] If secularism is an ideology and means the literal

[6] See Harvey Cox, *The Secular City* (New York, 1966); Karl Rahner, "Theological Reflections on the Problem of Secularization," *Theology of Renewal* vol. 1, L. K. Shook, editor (New York, 1968), pp. 167–192; R. Martin Goodridge, "Relative Secularization and Religious Practice," *Sociological Analysis,* 30 (1968), pp. 122–135.

death of God, Jesus, and all religion, it is an unverifiable exaggeration. But secularization can be simply the process by which the world through the anthropocentric activity of man and his technology shifts the emphasis in the religious and holy away from superficial things to essentials. In this sense, secularization demands the recognition of God's total transcendence, the need for Jesus Christ to be not just verbally but ontologically the Word of God, the obligation of the Church never to let cultural forms obscure the essence of its life. It allows the believer to be a free and mature human being, recognizing the potential and challenge that authentic Christianity places before him. A pluralistic, secular (but not secularistic) society can, paradoxically, be the milieu of a particularly vital and mature Catholic faith.

(7) *Person and Community* Perhaps because of the anxieties of living in technological, autonomous, mobile, artificial societies, or perhaps through the discovery of the reality of the person over against the institution or system, Americans have come to a keen awareness of the value of the person. The person has potential, individuality, and life, qualities Christianity from the New Testament to Aquinas made central. Allied with these is the need for real community to develop the potential of persons.

CHARISMS AND RELIGIOUS LIFE[7]

Religious share a common vocation with all Christians, stemming from their baptismal commitment. There are different ways of living out this commitment. This diversity and variety within the Christian community was emphasized by Paul in his first letter to the Corinthians.

[7] See Mark Scannell, *Charism and Renewal in Religious Life*, M.A. Dissertation, Dubuque, Iowa, 1969, unpublished; "Meaning in Religious Life," *Sisters Today* 40 (1968), pp. 7–12.

A vocation to the religious life is an individual call which is accompanied by the offer of grace to live it out. In the Acts of the Apostles Christianity is referred to as "the Way" (Acts 9:2, 24:14), but there are differences in living the Way. Seeking to answer the question of the place of religious life within the Church, Vatican II stated:

From the point of view of the divine and hierarchical structure of the Church, the religious state of life is not an intermediate one between the clerical and lay states. Rather, the faithful of Christ are called by God from both these latter states of life so that they may enjoy this particular gift in the life of the Church and thus each in his own way can forward the saving mission of the Church.[8]

Religious life does not belong to the hierarchical structure of the Church, but it enters into the life and saving mission of the Church.

The Spirit dwells in the Church and in the hearts of the faithful as in a temple (cf. 1 Cor. 3:16, 6:19). In them He prays and bears witness to the fact that they are adopted sons (cf. Gal. 4:6; Rom. 8:15–16 and 26). The Spirit guides the Church into the fullness of truth (cf. Jn. 16:13) and gives her a unity of fellowship and service. He furnishes her and directs her with various gifts, both hierarchical and charismatic, and adorns her with the fruits of this grace (cf. Eph. 4:11–12; 1 Cor. 12:4; Gal. 5:22).[9]

Religious life exists within the Church in the charismatic area. Is religious life a part of the structure of the Church or is it a phenomenon within the structure of the Church? If it were a part of the structure, it would be the result of "divine" institution and would have a permanent quality to it—as does, for example, the episcopacy. Religious life is a phenomenon within the structure of the Church and has a more fragile quality.

8 Vatican II, *Dogmatic Constitution on the Church*, 44.
9 *Ibid.*, 4.

56

Because it is charismatic, religious life is not a purely human phenomenon—like the curia or acolytes. Religious life is a constant, existential manifestation of the Church, testifying to the presence and the working of the Holy Spirit in the Church. A charism is a gift given by the Spirit to men which manifests and reveals God's presence among us, and this gift is given for the common good. Some gifts of the Spirit or charisms are given to men and women to found and to join religious communities. The life of each sister, brother, priest is a response to a particular charism. There is no general vocation to religious life, just as a founder is not given a general vocation to found any religious community. Charisms are personal and result from an individual's relationship to God. A general charism to do or be something would lessen and even diminish the importance of the person. A person is not a friend to others in general but a friend to specific individuals. Within an individual's relationship to God are many potential powers to live his Christian life. Just as the original founder received an individual charism to found a new religious community, the religious of today has also received an individual call or charism to join a particular community. One of the reasons why the charism of the founder is institutionalized is so that others may join this community throughout history. The initial charism of the founder is concretized and kept alive through new members of the religious community—not through rules or biographies.

Charisms in members form the basis of the community. Each of the members possesses unique talents and gifts, and community is not meant to be a life based on uniformity but on a common internal unity which creates differences arising from the uniqueness of each. To equate unity and community (or even charism) with uniformity is deadening the following of Christ.

The notion of charism is basic to religious life, and yet its full theology—its power and individuality—remains to be worked out. Radical renewal expects the charisms of each of the members to become more active and alive. The Church and a particular religious community are like a human body. They need structural organization, yet like the human body, they must be free—free for charisms. If charisms are suppressed, churches and religious communities will become inflexible and lifeless . . . and will appear dead.

COMMITMENT TO APOSTOLIC COMMUNITY: BACK TO ESSENTIALS

It is significant that like so much of Catholic theology, the understanding of Christian vows to apostolic community remained unchanged for decades if not centuries. Perhaps we can trace the ossification of the theology of the vows to an unlikely pair: Martin Luther and Ignatius of Loyola. Luther's experiences of the religious life in the somewhat frightening years of the Late Middle Ages show many of the negative aspects of a life forcibly turned inward and legalized. It is significant that most religious today who watch a performance of John Osborne's play not only understand but at some moments identify with the portrayal of the ambiguous religious life into which Luther entered. Despite the shattering effects of Wittenberg and Trent, many apects of this religious life—inferior to the more creative and open centuries surrounding Francis and Dominic—lasted even into the United States after World War II. There is no need to describe the genius of Loyola's ideas about new forms of the religious life; they dominated most orders and congregations—for men and women—which were founded from his lifetime onward. Yet, their understanding of obedience and community, their theologies of prayer and liturgy were (necessarily!) one-sided. This implies neither a criticism of Ignatius Loyola in the sixteenth century nor of the Jesuits and related congregations today. It simply returns us to the revolutionary crisis of our times and to recognizing the necessary dialogue between being-a-Christian and being-an-American in the 1970's. The following pages attempt to rediscover the essentials: community, poverty, celibacy, authority.

To locate the political, social, and communal dimensions of religious life through old and new structures is a large task. A complete hermeneutic of ideas such as "vow" and "poverty" from an American perspective has not been attempted, although this would be valuable. Some writers have pointed to it; Gabriel Moran remarks on poverty and the United States' government's "war on poverty."[10] Joseph Mulligan shows how a young person totally committed to peace, to protesting for peace to the point of prison, must live much the same as one bound by the traditional three vows: "The draft resister must have his priorities straight. He must value morality, integrity, conscience, faithfulness to God, and sensitivity to his brothers more than material comforts . . . conformism. . . . The draft resister must be willing to risk the future in faithfulness to God, for a record of felony . . . will be detrimental to his future opportunities for employment in many fields."[11] Obedience in the field of human social protest is more "secular" than religious, and consequently more vertical. "Obedience and loyalty to the one true God, whether He is named explicitly or not, necessarily prevents that idolatrous subordination of the person to the nation that passes for patriotism in our time."[12] This kind of re-interpretation is extremely important. It takes away the phony façade from houses where no serious encounter for Christ ever takes place. The gap between "religious" and "laity" is narrowing, and declining credibility gaps force Christian institutions to assess their meaning

---

[10] Gabriel Moran and Maria Harris, *Experiences in Community* (New York, 1968), pp. 153ff.

[11] J. E. Mulligan, S.J., "Religious Life and Civil Disobedience," *Review for Religious,* 28 (1969), pp. 445–451.

[12] *Ibid.*

again and again. The following fundamental outline may ground more such studies.

Community[13]

There is a new burst of awareness and desire for community both within and without the Church. The need for community is deep in the heart of man. Religious and apostolic life cannot find its source, realization, or sign value simply in the fact that a group of men or women dress alike and perform certain ritual actions together. Human relations are too profound, too important for this superficial bond to suffice. Why do religious live in community? In some way it must be to enable and to enrich a human, Christian, apostolic, and celibate life. Each of these aspects calls for community and must find it or be frustrated. For the present generation, isolated and made anxious by advancing technology, community is essential. A new view of religious life must emphasize its importance and its roots in the New Testament.

Community exists to help the person develop as a person, to help the Christian develop as a Christian. Community must be an adult familial community, for this is basic to man. If a man does not create one through marriage, he must find another form, for man cannot live totally alone and live healthily. Religious community life, like the Christian individual, is a place where nature and grace meet. The charisms of the Spirit, the times, the heritage of the order, the psychological needs of persons are aspects highlighting the importance of community. Community supports the individual in his aspostolate; it gives him direction and encouragement. But community is not just

[13] Many of the ideas in the following pages are derived from a paper prepared by a group of Midwestern Dominicans entitled "Towards a Theology of the Dominican Life in the United States Today."

the backdrop for activity; it is essential to effective Christian life and apostolate. Apostolate and community are correlatives. Neither can be defined without the other. We are involved in a communal apostolate and an apostolic community. We do not yet know how the rather recent rediscovery of the importance of community will profoundly affect community life, but we do know that for the United States and the American life-style this rediscovery is important, perhaps more important (and more advanced) than for Europe.

The previous form of routine, joint prayer (which is not the same as communal prayer), tolerant charity, frustrating or limiting obedience was insufficient. It often led to seeking a "family" outside of the priory rather than bringing friends into our family. A juridical description of community is insufficient, since community is primarily human and Christian, a psychological and socio-theological reality. Law can neither form nor direct true community; it can only give a very few boundaries beyond which community could not exist. From these legal lines to real community is a long road, but it is a road which Christians could begin to traverse if they would emphasize grace, not law.

If the Church is a microcosm of the world, the religious community is a microcosm of the society in which it lives. The religious community should be a model or type of Christian community. By its very existence in communal sharing and dedication to preaching the gospel, the religious community shows it is not the world. But the religious community is in the world. It shares in human communities—in their life and in their structures. By baptism and vows we look to a special fulfillment beyond the merely social community of family and city. This is possible, however, only if we listen closely to the insights of the gospel, to the Church, and to the contributions of the secular sciences. Psychology can be seen as a *praeparatio evangelica* for healthy community life, for charity, maturity, honesty, joy, and dedication. We must learn what is the correct size for

61

a community of men or of women, as determined by social and psychological studies; how a community can best be directed; what is the importance of work; whether one community needs a single apostolic goal or whether a community can be pluralistic. Neither theology nor canon law have all the information; social psychology and structural planning must help. We will see below how community is the source of authority. The superior exemplifies the spirit of the community, inspiring and coordinating the activities of the community. He is not primarily a secretary, a bookkeeper, or a control center for daily life.

The community should be open because Christian love is open; the community is mature and the superior a guide rather than a controller because this reflects the Christian (beyond the Jewish) idea of God. No closed community is happy. Jesus Christ was not closed in upon himself. Christian community-apostles must not only be intellectually open, but emotionally and psychologically ready to change, to risk. To be such, the religious community must be physically open to the communities it borders. Religious communities cannot be fortresses, for these are anachronistic. Rather, they must be dynamic centers of the Christian prophetic word engaging in conversation and cooperation with the world. Privacy and silence have a purpose, but they are not absolutes; they are ordained to dialogue and mission, and so cannot object to reasonable openness.

Young people today are realistic and idealistic without accepting ideologies. The world offers the young great benefits today, and not just "materialistic" or "worldly" pleasures. There is an enormous amount of sacrifice and dedication displayed at this time in America. Yet, this is a time when vocations are dropping disastrously. Young people expect a vocation to the religious, evangelical, and missionary apostolate to include a realistic appraisal of what it can or cannot accomplish. There are two consequences of this. First, religious life cannot act as though it has some arcane, always effective knowledge and methodology

62

which turns people into holy and effective apostles. Secondly, we expect that religious life, like every life, must be lived from day to day. Vows are a beginning of a life, not an end. The original commitment to work and sacrifice for the apostolate must be present when a person is fifty years old as well as when he is twenty-five. If this drive dies out, how can we say that life continues in its negative shell? Steps must be taken to insure constant renewal in the life of each individual just as secular society works through continuing education to render its own activities effective.

Vows as Commitment to Community and Apostolate

The vows are directed toward community membership and activity. Since they are acts of persons, they have personal implications such as lasting celibacy, personal mortification and denial, communal sharing, and so forth. But the community dimension can no longer be eclipsed by the personal; it is the community way of life which asks for celibacy; it is a particular level of apostolic efficiency and potential which requests poverty; and obedience is basically not the submission to one man's direction in the details of life, but the entrance into a community with its own necessary leadership. Vows are a lasting commitment to service through community for the Kingdom of God. Obedience is commitment to community; poverty exists for service, peace, and equality; chastity is essential to this kind of dedication.

Because of the importance of the New Testament and an individual's commitment, we must have a biblical theology of commitment-in-vows, and, further, a sociology and psychology of them as well. The vows are not restraints but liberating influences. Are the vows the same as every or any commitment to a religious community? Do they have positive sign value today, as the Council demands they should? Does their nomenclature get in the way? We must be wary of stating a theology of vows in terms of exclusivism or triumphalism. We cannot take for granted our identification of virginity with virtue, poverty with righteousness, or the religious life with a higher state. The vows, like the religious life, cannot be absolutes, for they are means.

How can Americans rediscover, emphasize, and explicate the goals toward which the vows tend? If these goals die out or escape achievement, the vows no longer have any real purpose. The keeping of a vow without any purpose or success is not in keeping with Jesus' religious thought. Vows are means to love, to zeal, to openness, to adaptation, to maturity, to Christian apostolic success, to service. Vows do not permit us to have no concern for the future of ourselves or our society, to have no interest in others, to withdraw, to escape decisions and responsibilites, persecution and defamation, to escape the necessity of worrying about life and livelihood, to ignore the effectiveness of our community and the Church. The purpose of the vows is to communicate Christ through a personal and communal life in God.

CELIBACY

A theology of religious celibacy avoids dualism. It never loses sight of the goodness of human emotions and sexuality, the permanent role sexuality plays in a balanced personality. Celibacy is not a means of not-getting-involved in the world, of "avoiding near occasions of sin." Celibacy is not a way of playing safe, nor are sins against chastity the most horrendous of the religious life, adding "malice" to sexual disorder. A sister's or priest's life can be a selfishness of great proportions. Celibacy must search seriously for its justification, and each must ask whether he justifies his living of a life which is not creative of human family; he asks this question not just once at perpetual vows but throughout his life.

It is not at all clear that Americans today are more involved in sexual immorality than in the past, although they are certainly barraged with the glorification of sexuality. Still, the seriousness of not sharing one's life with another human being, the potential ambiguity of sexual abstinence, and the gift of creating a family should not be set aside easily. Does celibate community as a commitment to Christian service have the theology and sign value for today it deserves? How do religious love in a human way? How is sexuality present in a love for the community and the world? Psychology must help to determine the dynamics and limitations of control and freedom in each individual, and the particular conditions which this or that province or house must take into account.

Celibacy allows for a certain level of Christian dedication to the apostolate and sanctity. It is academic to ask whether this is better or best, since only the individual with his God-given vocation has a "place" in the sight of God. This allows (it does not insure or cause) dedication to: (1) many persons rather than a few; (2) areas of work which are dangerous or demanding in an exceptional way; (3) an intensity of work in quality and quantity. Celibacy is connected with the revolutionary, missionary, and suffering nature of the Christian apostolate insofar as the celibate preacher of the gospel can go where a family cannot. With poverty, it allows a certain economic and social independence, a freedom from political or economic systems which may perversely harm human life and development.

POVERTY

Poverty is not simply the absence of normal or special consumer goods. Amid growing American affluence, poverty is an

65

evil. Our American mentality is intent upon its elimination. A long time ago Aquinas realized that a Christian "vow" of poverty had to be a dubious thing, since poverty is an evil. Christian poorness can have value in America as a sign of Christian eschatology and as an identification with the downtrodden and persecuted. In the present social and political upheavals within the United States, it has become clear that some religious who "practiced poverty" (sometimes in ludicrous detail) at the same time possessed a mentality which was unsympathetic to the poor. Poverty must be seen, then, as a sign of the worldly and transcendent kingdom of God, of the "already" and "not yet" of the Christian mission.

There are three aspects of poverty within the religious life, aspects which must be constantly tested as to whether they have a contemporary voice and to whether they are kept in the right balance. (1) Poverty of the individual and community must be proportionate to the particular apostolate and community. Poverty must smooth the road to effective apostolate and Christian service. We must not let privileges, traditions, and "contacts" little by little lead us away from all service to the poor and persecuted. (2) Poverty has sign value: it frees us for work for the Kingdom of God which is coming; it proclaims our faith in divine providence and in the power of Christ to become the center of the evolving world. Our faith in Christ above and within the world is active now and in the future. (3) Poverty frees us for work among persons and proclaims the primacy of the personal, Christian, spiritual over the material. Wealth is power; but poverty affirms faith in another power, a power which is ultimately greater because it influences not mountains or machinery but persons and ideas.

Vatican II emphasized the importance of real sign value to poverty, the importance of *personal* poverty and of *corporate* poverty. The latter demands real financial sharing on a national and international level as *integral* to the living of the vow of poverty. The *Pastoral Constitution on the Church in the Modern World* asks that we take up dialogue with the world as it is. With regard to the economic dimensions, we see that technology has given us means of great value and importance. Wealth is good, and the assumption—dominant from the origins of man—that poverty and sickness are inevitable and frequent is now questioned by American youth, scientists, and polity. The correct direction of this nation's wealth and power would be a greater by-product of our dedication to poverty than our supercilious contempt of all who possess or study wealth. In short, are we "using" our poverty for people?

Poverty not only allows us to be especially dedicated to apostolates, but demands that we employ time and energy well in our areas of work. Poverty can mean employing secretaries, jet travel, electronic media, and so forth in order to reach in a year (or a day) thousands more than Paul or Dominic contacted in a lifetime. On the personal level, poverty can easily be rendered moribund by establishing a life where all needs are filled immediately within a fully ordered house. Poverty means lack of security but trust in God. Poverty should prepare religious for living in the present era where the models and concepts of the religious life are being hotly debated and seriously questioned. Poverty and faith are correlates; poverty and routine or unchallenged life are contradictions. Poverty rejects any defense of the past which turns priories, publications, apostolates, liturgies, and so forth into the displays of a museum. This is especially true in the United States where we have practically no past and where our mentality is future oriented.

Very practically, poverty is a commitment to community life. The American religious wants to know where and who this community is. He takes for granted his right to have some information on how the large amounts sacrificed or earned are being spent. The United States' Church has experienced many cases of poor planning, excessive construction of buildings, unneeded apostolates, waste or diffusions of sums of money. The Christian who commits himself to poverty in a community has an obligation to see that that community itself is not sinning against poverty, and clearly superiors must answer not only to God but to the members of the community who freely offer their earnings. The spirituality and life of religious in the area of poverty are not helped but rather frustrated by remote, corporate decisions on the spending of money. Can we not expect that a religious who sees money wasted will hesitate to remain within the community or to continue his work and sacrifice?

OBEDIENCE

Thomas Aquinas emphasized the theological importance of God's creation and agents. God acts directly in his world rarely. Similarly, obedience is not just a personal relationship to God, and a superior never fully takes the place of God or Jesus Christ. Obedience is a commitment to God's kingdom revealed to us in Christ as present in a special ecclesial community. Obedience like authority involves community.

Americans are raised in the Anglo-Saxon tradition of law. This tradition is often almost in contradiction to certain Roman and European philosophies of law. The British and American legal mentality looks to a minimum of laws and a maximum of obedience; this is allied to equity but does not tend toward dispensation. Clearly the spirit of religious constitutions of the past and the Code of Canon Law stem from another philosophy. That is why the Constitution of the United States with 190 years of amendments fills only a few pages, while the laws of the community of "Christian freedom" total thousands. This national difference will influence American reaction to laws, authority, and obedience in the religious life.

The purpose of authority is not to rule over the details of the life of children, but to enable their maturation and sanctity. Adulthood, participation, and decision-making can and should belong to all the members of a community in a society where political maturity is taken for granted. From the point of view of charisms, the Spirit cannot be relegated to the mind of the superior, nor will educated Christians accept the point of view that the will of the superior is always God's positive (as contrasted with His permissive) will. Education and adulthood render implausible the neo-Platonic idea that the superior informs the inferiors because he always knows—intellectually or theologically—more than they do. Rather, the superior brings to focus the will of the community when it is holy and reasonable, or solves dilemmas presented by opposing parties. Traditions of democracy, initiative, consensus, and Aquinas' emphasis on nature with grace have been obscured by later spiritual theologies.

There is a crisis in communities over whether different points of view exist, or whether bureaucratic control can yield to political maturity. Today's crisis of obedience cannot be solved by more laws, stricter censures, and tighter controls. This will only lead to the sin of forcing schism and apostasy. Mature Christians cannot renounce their own consciences over what seems erroneous or insignificant. The crisis of obedience shows that a new kind of person is emerging in the Western world. He is quite different from either the medieval peasant or the European bourgeois. His education, social responsibility, and creative initiative can either be used within the community, or *he* can be rejected. But he will not choose to live as a nonperson, stripped of his own existence and potentiality—for neither common sense nor Christian virtue would suggest that he do so.

There is a crisis in the Church today centering in the *realization of authority*. This is not simply "a crisis of authority." What is at issue is not that authority, even that infallible authority

69

exists, but *how* it exists. This crisis is of great extent and needs a *solution* rather than a repression. The crisis is stimulated by the ever increasing role played by the mass media in Church affairs, by Vatican II's theology of collegiality, and by the transition of the Church from a feudal or immigrant power to a vital stimulus within a pluralistic society. The crisis is particularly acute in the United States due to our lack of roots in the past history of the Church, to the American political mentality, and to the tension arising from past attempts to merge these two. The future should not be allowed to witness a growing division between our standard style of administration on the one hand, and the majority of religious, especially the young, on the other.

The New Testament recognizes even within its normative pages a certain pluralism in Church forms. An example of this is found in St. Paul's First Letter to the Corinthians, chapters twelve through fourteen. Different gifts are given to different members of the Church by the same Spirit. Every member of the Church does not have the same function, just as each part of the body does not have the same function. Though these members have different rules, a unity still exists from the members' relationship to Christ. There is a diversity in the Church, but it is a diversity which is unified in Christ. All of these gifts are given for the building of the Church. In this view of the Church given by St. Paul, there is definitely an emphasis on a plurality in Church forms, but a pluralism which is unified in Christ.

Yet, the division, isolation, and frustration felt by many religious do exist. Where do they come from? Central authority often seems to be irrelevant. Why? Perhaps because it offers negative laws *post factum* rather than leadership before and during the moments of decision. This kind of authority is frustrating to those who have not been consulted and whose circumstances militate against the decision taken; it is irrelevant to many who may prefer real community and effective apostolate, even when there is risk involved in choosing these, to belonging to a long-established group. The following three ideas are guidelines by which to measure practical decisions on renewing the personal realization of lasting commitment. New structure for administration will be discussed later.

(1) *Charity* Charity is primary. Past constitutions have given the impression that holiness and charity come infallibly from obedience. Experience teaches that this is not true. Love for the community and the individuals in it must have a certain primacy over systems, machinery, and political goals. Love is prior to obedience and is the original cause of obedience. The present crisis will not be solved without a greater emphasis on love for the individual person.

(2) *Freedom* It is the purpose neither of the vow of obedience nor of government to plan each individual's days and life. There should be an atmosphere freely to be lived in, not a minute horarium to be conformed to. Vatican II's *Pastoral Constitution on the Church in the Modern World* begins with man, his dignity, and freedom; religious should not be afraid to follow that example. The purpose of authority should be to offer maximum help with minimum legislation.

(3) *Community* Freedom, education, and personal maturity are some of the catalysts for today's crisis in religious community. Until we are accustomed to collegial decisions at all levels, we will have anguish and potential death in American religious institutes. Three things are involved in the government of a community vis-à-vis the new problems: the struggle for real community life; the necessity of being pluralistic without sacrificing heritage or unity; and the desire for apostolate corresponding to personal needs and exigencies of society and of community.

We certainly do not have all the answers about forming this new community life on either the personal or the structural level. Clearly some things must go and others stay. But we must strive toward what is mentioned immediately above, for

71

these things are fundamental to what religious life claims to be. The struggle for them is itself good. Complaints about impending doom and disaster fail in Christian hope. The struggle is evangelical, since the vocation and following that Jesus preached include uncertainty. In the past we created a world where we conquered the future by avoiding it, by being static. We must not be afraid of uncertainty or risk and even danger in evaluating and living life. Today, we do not really have conflict within the development of representation and pluralism in government; we have a conflict as to whether pluralism and collegiality should be allowed to exist at all. This conflict is disastrous, for new forms of realizing authority in religious community can be combated in America only at the price of a Pyrrhic victory, the decline of religious life.

Political philosophy tells us that there are two questions in the renewal of political structure: (1) What is your model of person? What kind of people are you dealing with? (2) In the light of what is best suited for these persons, who decides and governs? In considering our political structures, have we overlooked the first question? In regard to the second, decision and consultation should penetrate into the community as far as they can. This is a principle not only of politics but of a Christian theology of virtue.

How are mature American religious to come to realize that representation and political discussion about the leadership and direction of the order is not evil? The Acts of the Apostles record discussion among the apostles. For an American, not to question, not to engage in political life, is to be immature. We must not allow the leaders of men and women religious (who are not on the same theological plane as bishops) to become persons who mix the sacred with the secular like kings of divine right. Some attempt must be made to open more lines of communication, to broaden the base of authority, to give the greatest possible representation, to recognize the responsibility of local communities for their lives, to allow for pluralism and even dissent—all within the context of religious obedience to those in office. How this is to be done without weakening authority is a challenging but far from insuperable question. To many from other cultures, the entire view may seem bizarre or even dangerous. However, it is a legitimate possibility within ecclesial religious life, and it is the normal and traditional political mentality of Americans. Actually, obedience will grow where love has primacy; zeal will become more intense where consultation (with or without final agreement) has made it feel worthwhile. While commitment to Christian community-apostolate is destroyed by depersonalization and autocracy, it is increased through openness and honesty.

4. Secularization and Community

THE two following chapters approach community and apostolate from the perspective of contemporary theological reflection. The theological approach presents few concrete answers but it is no less necessary. It gives fundamental guidelines, and, if it is truly theological, it tries to scout out the future facing the People of God. Harvey Cox describes the theologian as standing on "the jagged edge where the faithful company grapples with the swiftest currents of the age."[1]

It belongs to contemporary theology, faithful to the gospel but studious of today's world, to create new dimensions for apostolate and community. An opening paragraph of the *Pastoral Constitution on the Church in the Modern World* is related to this:

Today, the human race is passing through a new stage of its history. Profound and rapid changes are spreading by degrees throughout the world. Triggered by the intelligence and creative energies of man, these changes recoil upon him, upon his decisions and desires, both individual and collective, and upon his manner of thinking and acting with respect to things and to people. Hence we can already speak of a true social and cultural transformation, a transformation which has repercussions on man's religious life as well.[2]

[1] Harvey Cox, "The Place and Purpose of Theology," *The Christian Century,* 83 (1966), p. 7.
[2] Vatican II, *Pastoral Constitution on the Church in the Modern World,* 4.

We have already seen how positive and inescapable catalysts from our American society cause upheavals within community and apostolate in religious life. Like theology and like the Church, religious life's profound process of renewal is a re-orientation from inwardness to outwardness, from long revered ideas to people and problems, from taking the past for granted to seeing the future as awesome.

DIALECTIC BETWEEN COMMUNITY AND APOSTOLATE

The religious life is neither community or apostolate, unless by those words we mean apostolic community or communal apostolate. The religious life is life lived within and between the two; it is like electricity which crackles out between these two poles of charge. I do not believe either can be described in constitutions or lived existentially in local communities without taking into full account the other. A community determines certain apostolates on a regional and local level; the apostolate will essentially determine the way of life, the encounter of prayer and liturgy. How can there be an abstract, universal community life which, unmodified by concrete life or apostolic circumstances, is lived independent of a variety of apostolates? The further delineation of this complex relationship remains for each group to work out creatively at various levels. The local religious team's life must allow for the development and satisfaction of creative, educated, mature Americans living in the 1970's—which means community life must be more than simply a backdrop for "jobs."

The development of the right balance for the new adult community life and for worthwhile apostolates of professionally trained Americans is crucial. For upon this depends, first, the perseverance of tens of thousands of religious who are con-

75

scientiously judging the value of their own religious life, and, secondly, the attraction of young people to each order or congregation. It is clear that young people are now little attracted by literature, abstract ideas, century-old heroes. They will not let "supernatural promises" cover up a life which seems to be impossible or suffocating (despite its inspiring origin and goal) because of a detailed and/or legalistic form. The young are attracted by concrete persons and what they are doing, by how they are living up to what they claim is important. Christian theology, when it is concerned with and listening to contemporary American society, can offer suggestions about the reality—oscillating between community and apostolate—the religious life.

Theology in conversation with the world and humanity enables us to develop the opening reflections of Vatican II's *Decree on the Appropriate Renewal of the Religious Life*. These urge "(1) a continuous return to the sources of all Christian life and to the original inspiration behind a given community and (2) an adjustment of the community to the changed conditions of the times." The principles offered as guide in such change are five: (a) the gospel is the origin and supreme norm of religious life; (b) a certain diversity among religious communities serves the needs of the Church's witness of holiness and apostolate best; (c) religious communities should participate in the life of the Church, fostering its objectives in such areas as scriptural studies, the liturgy, teaching, and "pastoral, ecumenical, missionary and social" apostolates; (d) communities should promote among their members an awareness of contemporary human conditions and of the needs of the Church; (e) interior renewal of spirit must accompany external structural renewal. All of this implies a twofold direction of renewal: toward the revolutionary vitality of the New Testament and toward the tensions and potentialities of contemporary culture.

The Directions of Contemporary Theology

Once we take the trouble to find out what theologians like Jürgen Moltmann, Harvey Cox, and Karl Rahner are talking about, we see that there are really four recurring themes of theological work today; language, future, secularization, and social change.[3] While our faith tells us that the world does not give us Christianity and that the world (the cosmos of John's gospel) both accepted and crucified the Incarnate Word, still it is the world and the people in it who determine the language and apostolic forms of the Church's mission. We have a mission from Christ, but a mission to the people alive today; we are in no way responsible for the past generations we cannot help, nor for the future peoples we will never see. We must understand, listen to, and learn from ourselves, from our world, from our fellow citizens of this one world how to live in religious community and how to preach effectively the Good News. Behind these four dimensions of theological work is a new understanding —emerging, not yet complete—of man and his many communities. The previous chapters described how these factors of a new personal and social theology influence the essentials of religious life. The dimensions of change for a better future and a radical critique of ideas and words give the initial impetus to these pages. *What is challenging our communities is the Western, particularly American process of secularization; what is challenging our apostolates is the new revolutionary demands of social change and the process of humanization* (which for Teilhard de Chardin has Christ as its source and focal point). We must ask what a Christian theology of secularization and social change can tell us about ourselves. Religious communities

[3] See Thomas F. O'Meara, "Where Is Theology Going?", *Thought*, 44 (1969), pp. 53–68.

do not escape being human communities of persons, and what is influencing all communities (not necessarily destroying them) is increased secularization. Similarly, the horizon of man's concern for his neighbor is social change. More and more he is called to work for the improvement of the community, the ghetto, the suburb, or the world. He is called to work for the community in its struggle for peace, for racial or economic justice, or for ecclesial renewal and representation.

Secularization and the Religious Community

Secularism and secularization are two quite different things. Secularism is an "ism," an ideology. If it means complete and unqualified acceptance and exaltation of the world, or if it means the identification of the Kingdom of God fully with social change, it is unacceptable to the Christian gospel. That is secularism. Secularization, however, is neutral. It is simply a process, a fact, a reality. It is dimension, the horizon of life in the West (and increasingly in other parts of the globe, for example, Tokyo). It finds its pacesetter in the United States. Secularization is the fact that the secular and not the religious (whether primitive sacred or Christian) dimension dominates our world. One way of realizing this is by contrasting our cities with European, urban, cathedral-dominated skylines; the difference is also evident in American mobility, technology, and communications. Harvey Cox writes:

The coming of the secular city supplies the new occasion. In the face of its coming, attitudes which have been brought along from yesterday must be discarded, and a new orientation which is in keeping with the new social reality must be initiated. Today the Gospel summons man to frame with his neighbor a common life suitable to the secular city. He responds by leaving behind familiar patterns of life that are no longer apropos and by setting out to invent new patterns.[4]

The secularization process makes man autonomous, makes his faith personal rather than institutional. It accepts technology rather than divine intervention as the explanation and the catalyst of day-to-day life. Does this affect the religious community? Yes. The apostolic religious community must know the secular world to which it is sent, sympathize with it, and learn from it. Our concern, our commission is not to preach a philosophy or a sociology, not a style of dress nor a form of entertainment, but the gospel. We cannot change the society in which we live in its basic, neutral, good contours; we dilute our apostolic efforts if we confuse all secular with evil, if we confuse the good aspects of the cosmos with the twisted or demonic ones.

The People of God, or divine community, cannot come into being without the human community, and human community, in fact, includes the divine community, whether or not it is actually recog-

[4] Harvey Cox, *The Secular City* (New York, 1966), p. 105. For the influence of American secularization on Christian communal life, we mention characteristics singled out by J. B. Metz in his analysis of faith viewing the world: (1) *Pluralism*. The believer must fully relate his faith to a pluralism of life forms. A pluralism of approaches and life-styles grows at the same time as a double world of sacred and secular is diminishing; (2) *Involvement in a World Not Permeated with Faith*. America never had a history of medieval Christianity, and secularization is not so new. Yet we expect to see the Christian present exclusively in certain institutions—churches, clubs, schools, social classes. We will have to learn that the Spirit is unchained and that Christianity is likely "to learn its most challenging ways from the world"; (3) *Ambiguous Secularity*. The world will become even more secular, more its own master, and the Christian attitude toward it must remain ambiguous, not unfree from pain at the new circumstances of faith/world. How is the secularization, the coming to age of the world, also its Christianization? (4) *Illusionless Hope and Persistence as the Christian Attitude*. The Christian must try to combine a powerful hope with a critical lack of illusions. The world needs and expects both. It expects from Christian communities hope and service as the fundamental dialectic, but it also implies criticism and lasting freedom from every establishment. *Theology of the World* (New York, 1969), pp. 42–50; see pp. 70–77.

nized. . . . This does not mean that the human community is the same as the divine community, because God is not totally defined by what is human, but he is present in man and manifests himself in man and in what is human. . . . Within the sphere of human action we are always and everywhere confronted with the God who chose to show himself and to be present among us in our own autonomous world. For this reason, a reflection upon human reality and its autonomy is a condition that must be fulfilled before we can understand the salvation proclaimed to us, which is the God become man.[5]

Those entering religious life are, and have been for some time, products of this process of secularization. This is especially true in America, for we American Catholics have lived until recently as a minority in the midst of a somewhat alien culture. (A Catholic theology of secularization may be easier to develop than a Protestant one.) The religious life should not be identical with "communities" of secular service, but it must correspond to the people involved in their existential-personal roots, that is, in the style of living, of thinking, in language, action, and thought-forms.

Gabriel Murray sees three types of religious: (1) the eschatological religious; (2) the modern personalist religious; (3) the secular religious.[6] These types are based upon mental patterns and lifestyles. The first has dominated for some time; it focuses on rules, on a totally "supernatural" way where anything can be tolerated—personal frustration or apostolic inefficiency—for the sake of an eschatological reward. This type is dying out. The eschatological element is strong, but the incarnational element is absent. A balance is missing.

The personalist religious is strongly influenced by existential

[5] W. Van der Marck, *Toward a Christian Ethic: A Renewal in Moral Theology* (Westminster, 1967), p. 69.

[6] G. B. Murray, "The Secular Religious," *Review for Religious*, 26 (1967), pp. 1047ff.; commenting on Murray is A. J. Weigert, "A Sociological Perspective on the 'Secular Religious,'" *Review for Religious*, 27 (1968), pp. 873ff. See Also R. Reichert, "Secularization and Renewal," *Review for Religious*, 27 (1968), pp. 852–70.

and personalist philosophies and is tired of the a-personal distinctions and excuses of an impersonal faith and community. This second category seems to be an important, but intermediate, stage in the development of the new kind of Christian apostle. Social concern and practical re-organization of highly influential structures can be lacking. There is a certain inability to relate achieved personalities to the wider concerns of society, nation, and world. And, the demand to renew society and Church with frequent frustration and a concomitant need for tactics and patience causes frustration and retreat here. Murray sees the secular religious as problem-centered. He or she is empirical and tough-minded, is skeptical of "isms," sees the liturgy as a bridge between community and world. The need for radically improved community life is recognized, but the entire effort of years cannot be placed there. In fact it is questionable how effort should be directed to personal development, since persons live in many wider worlds. "To this extent the third type of religious is a-religious. He *is* secular, he *is* a-religious and he is a Catholic Christian. He is thing-oriented, job-oriented, service-oriented and people-oriented . . . "

Placide Gaboury develops Murray's secular religious in the direction of urban pluralism. He draws on sociologists like Louis Wirth, Nels Anderson, George Sommel, Lee Taylor, and Arthur Jones to study the horizon of city life. It is first of all mobile, demanding a high capacity of adaptation. "The sophisticated character of metropolitan psychic life becomes understandable as over against small town life which rests upon more deeply felt and emotional relationships. These latter are rooted in the more unconscious layers of the psyche and grow most readily in the steady rhythm of uninterrupted habituations."[7] City life, secondly, is neutral, impersonal, competitive, anonymous—inviting and even presupposing tolerance. There is a certain

---

[7] P. Gaboury, "The Secular Religious and Pluralism," *Review for Religious*, 28 (1969), p. 615.

"blasé" attitude due to the multiplicity of events, situations, and persons. Gaboury feels that today's communities can survive and be healthy only through a pluralistic mentality. "The personalistically inclined religious will find it harder than the secular religious to live on a pluralistic basis, and the European (especially Latin) personalist might find it still harder, since his concept of pluralism seems less attuned to the pluralism of highly urbanized and technological society." What results from this pluralistic attitude is a necessary ambiguity toward the world: working for it, yet critical of it. "He is critical and on the alert, as though he saw things from the outside, bearing in mind the historical implications of a way of doing, and remaining open to every changing application of basic trends. In this sense, the Christian, and in particular, the religious, could be one who contests the established order inasmuch as it is taking itself too seriously, that is, taking for absolute and necessary what is provisional, relative, disposable, and contingent. He is one who has outgrown the absoluteness of either/or attitudes. He is geared for an Ultimate rather than an Absolute Now. This could be why he is capable of total involvement and yet remains wary of a here and now absolute."[8]

Secularization as the horizon of American life is affecting religious community in two ways: the secularization of things and new kinds of persons.

The Secularization of Things

Most Protestant and Catholic theologians are agreed that we are at the end of a long process which de-sacralizes things; de-sacralization of things allows the emergence of the Spirit of God and the freedom of man. Judaism and Christianity were crucial catalysts here. The Old Testament forbade idols, preached

[8] *Ibid.*

82

one transcendent God, took Israel out of a theo-monarchy in Egypt, discouraged through prophets the elevation of kings or priests. Clearly Jesus interiorizes religion, allowing only a few external signs to remain (meal, community, water), and they are subordinate to grace, Spirit, and the human person. The preaching of Jesus, the writings of John and Paul are a constant insistence upon the value of the individual, the otherness of God, and his love for men in Christ, and the definitive end of all superstition or idolatry of things.

It is a characteristic of Catholic religious communities (in contrast with Protestant sects) to discover their mission in the world. The Benedictine monasteries became educational and cultural centers. Vincent de Paul could write of his "new nuns" in seventeenth-century France: "You have as a monastery the house of the poor, for your cell wherever you pray, for a chapel the parish church, for a cloister the streets of the city, for a cloister obedience, for a grill the fear of God, for a veil holy modesty." Secularization lets us see that the world is good, see its goodness in a new way: hospitals, cars, homes, air-conditioning, vitamins, etc. We are also being tuned in on the de-sacralization of what is left of religious buildings, religious clothes, religious things. Thomas Aquinas would have told us that the only "sacred things" in the New Covenant are the sacraments. They are drawn from everyday living and must retain a sign value, that is, they must *work* as Christian signs.[9] Certainly the value of religious signs is changing. Some old values and new values will remain, for the sacred, the holy perdures in new, more hidden forms. What secular man sees is that sacred things and sacred signs and even sacred persons must be judged pragmatically, on their merits within the sphere of active Christianity. For instance, superiors have little or no automatic claim to God's charismatic favor if they do not on their own try to discover in the community his will and his love. The congrega-

---

[9] *Summa theologiae*, III, q. 60, a. 2; q. 61. a. 1.

tion's age-old taboos dating from the eighteenth or thirteenth centuries must prove themselves, or be set aside as wasteful. Obedience is now seen as primarily a commitment to a community which like all communities has authority. Any claim by an individual to constant wire-tapping of the divine will is dismissed as superstitious. Nor can we facilely identify the will of God with the will of superiors when this will is manifestly uninformed or erroneous. God does not will the mismanagement of people, or if he does, it falls into the same general ontological category as his "willing" of deformed children. So, the secular person often demands a better Christian theology, and both the gospels and the secular thrust frequently ask for the same thing.

New Kinds of Persons

A secular society produces many new, valuable characteristics in people; we can single out only a few.

The first is *education*. Our society survives only on massive and intensive education. Education is the greatest growing industry in the United States; it is already clear education must encompass the lifetime of an individual. Our society's educated members must have creativity and competency to survive. These two factors, education and creative competency must be given adequate room in the community if it is to effectively touch upon the society in which we live.

A related characteristic is *political involvement*. We are no longer Europeans or immigrants. We take maximum political involvement for granted. No adult, educated American is going to place his or her life permanently in the hands of an elder clique even for the sake of Christ. For who knows whether Christ now wills this for the 1970's? Community involvement must correspond to political capability and expectation. It must be seen that the function of political criticism and the desire for political improvement does not necessarily imply sin or community betrayal. Superiors, especially on the provincial and national level, cannot retain the aura of consecrated office-holders where the realms of sacramental grace and effective government are mixed. Not only is political maturity a function of normal Americans, theology itself is heading in this direction. Theologians call for a "political theology." Its starting point is the Incarnation. Jesus Christ by his very existence affirms what is authentically human; by his mystical-corporal existence, the Church, he shows that Christianity is neither an individual nor a club, neither an earthly state nor a heavenly paradise. J. B. Metz writes:

Political theology seeks to make contemporary theology once again aware of the suit pending between the eschatological message of Jesus and the reality of political society. It stresses that the salvation proclaimed by Jesus is permanently concerned with the world, not in the natural cosmological sense, but in the social and political sense, as the discerning and liberating element of this social world and its historical process.[10]

Freedom, peace, justice, hope—these are neither purely political nor purely religious matters. Peace is not just a marginal, worldly issue for Christianity, nor is governmental politics capable of fully embracing and achieving peace. So, political theology is concerned with Christian maturity in creating a better human environment. Meanwhile, the religious community cannot afford to be an island of European, nineteenth-century, other-worldly isolation or retardedness in the face of this new current of politics and theology.

This leads us to the wide but important characteristic of

[10] J. B. Metz, "The Church's Social Function in the Light of a 'Political Theology,' " in *Concilium: Faith and the World of Politics,* 26 (New York, 1968), pp. 2–18.

involvement. Young people today are not interested in ideology but they are idealistic. They are not interested in the great deeds of long dead saints but they are interested in what people now are doing. They look not for passive imitation rewarded in heaven some decades hence but for involvement risking joy and sorrow. Whether this is, as Marshall McLuhan says, part of the re-orientation of our minds to new electronic patterns, it is a rediscovery of the evangelical spirit. The gospel tells us relatively little about heaven, little about God, but a great deal about serving other people in risky and sacrificing situations right now. Involvement should be broad: involvement in choice of apostolate, in decisions, involvement with people, with the others in the community. It means finding a new form of community life which breaks down façades and fears, and allows a charity and honesty closer to real friendship. Freedom, involvement, and friendship are as important to religious life as they are significant in today's society. The theologian is concerned with an ethic which allows the individual to be truly human, truly Christian in the face of all of the systems which threaten to make him an automaton. How often we heard the religious life as described precisely as such: a dehumanizing agency. More than ever, the presumption must be in the other direction.

CHRISTIAN COMMUNITY WITHIN
WORLD COMMUNITY

At one o'clock, the voice of Mission Control told the astronaut to "head on up the ladder," and announced that Neil Armstrong had been on the surface of the moon slightly more than two hours. In New York City, the rain was beating down steadily, but only when the hatch of the landing vehicle was closed eleven minutes later, did the last diehard spectators turn away. . . . Then people by the hundreds began streaming toward Fifth Avenue. Behind them, like an unblinking eye, the NBC screen still showed a picture of the LEM sitting at

Tranquility Base. The astronauts were safe inside and the moon walk was over, but almost everyone kept looking back over his shoulder through the downpour, as if to reassure himself that what he had seen with his eyes had really taken place upon the moon.

Donald Meany, a vice president of NBC News Division, while monitoring the first pictures from the moon, remarked: "One thing I think this is doing is bringing people together. The picture is going everywhere in the world by satellite. I hear they're getting a great picture in Bucharest. And in *Belgrade.* And, you know, nobody has the inside track on seeing these pictures. The scientists in Houston, the President of the United States, all of us in this room, perhaps Serbian peasants—they're all seeing the same fantastic live pictures at the same time . . . . Maybe that holds something pretty good for all of us."[11]

After the moon walk it began to dawn on many people that it was not completely satisfactory only to compare the cost of the Apollo project and the possible use of the money among the poor of the nation. The use of this money for social improvement (versus its multiplication in industry and invention) lost its initial emotional power before an ever stronger "mythical" discovery. For the first time in history a large segment of the human race was united, really united in hope and thrill, but also united in a world-wide television network, an artificial environment of glass eyes and electronic ganglia, united before the emerging picture of man reaching the moon. This "transcendental" electronic union of man looking at the surface of the moon was, certainly, as unique an historical event as the landing itself.

Vatican II uses the word "sign" in two, at first unrelated, ways in speaking of the "new" in the Church and religious life. It speaks of the "signs of the times" and it speaks of each Christian community being a real eschatological sign. These usages indicate that it is impossible to speak of Christian com-

[11] From the report of *The New Yorker* (July 26, 1969), p. 30.

munity except in terms of how community is viewed and exists in the world. The New Testament does indeed have a message about events, persons, and history, but this kerygma is destined to be a power in the ongoing history of creation, promising an eschaton and parousia which do not involve the destruction of creation. A sign necessarily involves reflection, dialogue; it is two-way. It is well applied to Christian life, because Christianity was never a religion or a sacred world apart from the world but a new life, a new creation, a basic faith-perspective, a loving service within the one world which exists. The Christian gospel was never meant to create a separate religious or sacred world. It did retire before Jewish and Roman persecution, but this ended with Gnosticism. Christianity was sectarian with regards to its immediate eschatology—for a few decades. But its worship, theology, kerygma were drawn from the stuff of life. It was precisely the this-worldly attitude of the Christians toward worship (not in temples but in terms of sacraments drawn from daily life: food, oil, water) which led the Romans to call them "*a-theistoi.*" The Middle Ages produced a Christian single world. St. Thomas synthesized the Bible with the daring, newly discovered works of Aristotle and his Arabic commentators. While he composed in Paris the different parts of the *Summa Theologiae* (synthesizing everything from Trinitarian processions to personal actions in a dynamic neo-Platonic framework), a few blocks away geniuses constructed in stone and glass at Louis IX's command the *Sainte Chapelle.* Its magnificent glass windows, occupying most of the wall space—a daring architectural feat, traced the continuity of a single sacred-secular kingship, beginning with Melchisedech (priest and king), culminating in Christ crowned with thorns, and living on in Louis, son of Blanche of Castille. Both were a world of diversity and unity in politics, discovery, faith, and worship.

The Reformation and the subsequent ages of Enlightenment, science, and discovery split this one world. Calvinism and Lu-

88

theranism were based upon such a division; Post-Tridentine Catholicism, fearful and divorced from the freedom to produce talented response, created pockets of Catholicism (not only in the Vatican but in schools and neighborhoods) to preserve a threatened faith. Now we are returning to a unified world. This is not the world of humanism, romanticism, scientism, communism, or Americanism; they have all been shown to be defective —precisely in their attitude toward man and death. We seek again the unity (but not the absorption) of the religious and the civic, of the sacred and the secular, where the Christian dimension in faith and active hope is disclosed precisely within our daily life and not in "another world" of church or ancient rite. This is indicated in liturgy where the complicated and colorful ancient rites, with antique vestments and movements (and much beauty and art), have yielded to informal worship in which life is celebrated and informed. It is shown in the multiplication of floating communities, seeking full and effective Christian community.

A World Seeking Unity

The world is seeking unity, but, children of original sin, we often are driven to what is good by our own magnification of evil. Problems of massive riots and suicidal wars born of the hunger and injustice of the discriminated families of man in the southern hemisphere press us to seek a unified world. Marshall McLuhan speaks of the world as a global village. But, to learn our new identity in one world of electronic media and multiple breakthroughs in education and productivity, will we have to go through a vast and horrendous educational process—war? War, McLuhan outrageously claims, is basically an educational experience during cultural transition. Of course, this time the education will be extremely expensive, so expensive as to perhaps destroy those involved. "Joyce was probably the only man ever to discover that all social changes are the effect of new technologies (self-amputations of our own being) on the order of our sensory lives. It is the shift in this order, altering the images that we make of ourselves and our world, that guarantees that every major technical innovation will so disturb our inner lives that wars necessarily result as misbegotten efforts to recover the old images."[12] The alternative "educational" process is creating and multiplying effective community. Peace, Augustine defines as the tranquility of order; for Aristotle the order of men implies living in society. Peace, then, implies an active and creative tranquility for the individual and the group coming from real community: living-with, communion, union, diversity and harmony—all are involved in the community of men.

Don't we already have community? Many communities? Or, from the opposite point of view, can the word *community* mean anything? Until recently, we have been used to speaking of community in certain places. Even this linguistic usage discloses something about today's crisis of community. We mention community in terms of the small town, the university community, the church. Political party, army units, religious orders have been examples of close knit groups where community could flourish. It is precisely these areas of "community" which today suffer the greatest inner strife and polarization. The university community witnesses violence and protest, with the intrusion of outside forces (political and military) over the issues of the university's responsibility to the community of students and the surrounding community. A journalist reported recently there are over 1,000 underground or floating church communities in America among Catholics. The parishes are split over religious education. We saw the effects of political community against political community at the Democratic convention of

---

[12] Marshall McLuhan, Quentin Fiore, *War and Peace in the Global Village* (New York, 1968), p. 5.

August 1968; nothing is more violent, apparently, than political division where there had been unity. Similarly, the playwright Arthur Miller said the lesson he had learned from the Democratic convention in Chicago was that the old hate the young. Do we have community anywhere? Perhaps a primary cause of the decline of vocations to the priesthood and religious life is that the diocese and religious communities present no unified image, and that the frustrations of younger Christian apostles are widely known by their potential followers.

Community, then, is threatened in America as it enters the 1970's. I use the word *threat* intentionally. I would call this threat a personal and political experience of all of us today. *Threat* has now expanded *anxiety*—the phenomenon which existential philosophy and drama saw in Western man after the Second World War. Martin Heidegger, Jean-Paul Sartre, and many others all called attention to this kind of man, man living in the age of anxiety. Now it seems we have entered a new age. Existential difficulties have expanded into social difficulties, into social, and structural problems. Man is no longer vaguely uneasy; rather—and we ourselves use the word so often—he is threatened. Like Faust, man has conquered nature, but he has problems with his companions. Who are they to be? God? Marguerite? Mephistopheles?

The individual yields to the future of society, the existential to the political. Anxiety came from a feeling of uneasiness about our own finitude. Threat comes from a vague intuition that the social structures which support us may collapse. We speak of being "threatened by other people." Why are older people threatened? Why are administrators or bishops threatened? Polarization in community is a result of feeling threatened, threatened not by individuals, but by the ideas and ways of life they may introduce. An individual can be dealt with. He can be fired, disciplined, imprisoned, bribed, controlled. But an individual cannot be so controlled, if he represents a social group

91

and the wave of the future. People are threatened because they feel that through groups or individuals comfortable social supports are being withdrawn; individuals are not coming toward us but strange waves of social change. Mayor Daley is not threatened by Tom Hayden of the SDS as an individual, but he is evidently terrified by political ideas Hayden represents. What is significant about the hippies is not that they return (Rousseau-like) to nature and take drugs—this is old—but that they form a new style of community and hope to spread this.

There is a union between new political and new theological ideas. They rouse the same feared implications. As in algebra it is possible often to discern ideas about three areas (for example, youth, Church, politics), if you know one of the factors. Going deeper, attitudes toward the new kind of films, toward the guitar as an instrument, toward the seminar method of teaching, toward changing images of masculinity are all correlates of this basic polarization between the threatening (with their little experience, no concrete program, and little to lose) and the threatened (with their "good life" to lose and with little practice in being free or thinking creatively). The pastor and the businessman are brought together in the John Birch Society because they fear the social changes which new ideas would bring about. And to some extent these changes would be radical, not because they are unfaithful to the Constitution of the United States and the New Testament, but because they would take these documents seriously. Above all, they would demand that political and theological power serve instead of manipulate! The over-all crisis in the world, with respect to community, is that quite different ideas about "human community" are emerging. These are not always within the framework of evolution and can be so diverse as to imply revolution. *Threat* is the tension resulting between different views of communal structure. No matter how liberal we may be, we fall asleep at night threatened by the future—which we suspect *must* be different.

92

The Christian Community: Threat and Promise

St. Paul says the word of God is a two-edged sword. In Johannine theology the world, the *kosmos*, is ambiguous. In the synoptics Jesus does not hesitate to place faith at the center of a dichotomy, to make it a cause of separation between men. The Christian community cannot enter into the contemporary situation as a celestial bringer of comforting relaxation. To announce a kerygma of easy solutions is to bring mockery upon the Church; to describe love and peace in the midst of hate and blood without showing the reconciliation of the two is so unrealistic as to appear effeminate and schizophrenic. The Christian community is both threat and promise. It is threat inasmuch as by its belief in an historical Incarnation (where the divine mysterious Logos becomes an individual man) and its confession of death being overcome in personal and historical resurrection, it affirms the value of each individual man, woman, and child. The Christian gospel is recognizing anew the political character of its message. An example of this is the beatitudes. Peacemaking is political, and it aims not initially at the interior peace of the mystic but at peace amidst real war. Hungering after justice and being poor are political realities. The idea of the Kingdom of God being ambiguous indicates that this Kingdom is both coming and already present; it is man's and God's. The Christian faith, which has learned again it must be more than a humanism, goes beyond the political dimension, both backward to the crucifixion and resurrection of Christ and forward to the possibility that the eschaton is dependent upon our human, social evolution.

Christianity is hope. It is a promise of the possibility of improvement and of peace. The Christian community with respect to forming its own community within the world is no longer defensive but active. Karl Rahner writes:

93

The Christian can truly achieve his own proper Christian being completely and fully only if he lives evidently and unconditionally in the present and in the future, not merely in the past. . . . The fact that being a Christian imposes a task within the world does not mean, of course, that "official" Christianity, i.e., the church itself, just therefore takes it into her own hands to develop and advocate a concrete program for an intramundane future derived solely from the principles which Christianity must alone advocate. . . . But Christians themselves must surrender to the future and regard it as their most proper tasks, even though this may expose them to uncertainty and risks.[13]

The Christian community will not "form" community through providing precise programs or demanding imitation. It works even in the formation of parochial or religious community for the wider communities of the world, for the "global village" the world is becoming. Christian community as a complex dialogue with the world is not static but creative and self-critical; it is honest about having or not having community. It is not an establishment but a witness—capable of new directions and evaluations.

There will, naturally, be many kinds of Christian communities: parochial and trans-parochial, floating and underground, temporal and lasting. The religious community is only one of these. The religious community has to investigate how it sees itself related precisely as Christian and American, evangelical and contemporary, to the search and need for community in the world. First of all, if it succeeds in arriving at community, it will have given the world a sign that community is possible. The hippies try to do this with flowers and honesty. Can it not be done with "grace"? Secondly, the prophetic voice of the Christian community, in and outside of its main apostolate, about what is happening to people in local communities is important. In a time of great change silence is the same as opposition.

[13] "Christianity and the New Man," *The Sacred and the Secular*, M. Taylor, editor (New York, 1967), pp. 100f.

Thirdly, much of the direction of Christian apostolate should be concerned with community. Education and *diakonia* are the foundations of community. The next chapter will discuss the relationship of our apostolates to new challenges in a revolutionary time. In our apostolates people and community must be put first or we make a mockery of the world's uncertain quest for community. It is precisely the control of people for materialistic and economic exploitation which is the great threat to world-wide community. If the religious communities continue to place buildings and institutions above people, they mock themselves. Any preference for uncriticized institutions with traditions afraid of and impotent within the new, simply says they prefer establishment to community.

5. Apostolate and Revolution

THE apostolate bridges the religious and the secular community. The dimension of the Christian and the holy, of service born of *agape* must be present in a religious community. It must be really present, not just "there" in a routine life-long commitment, in rules, or in a group of negative recluses praying routinely. It must be present as a sign to the world as Vatican II reiterates. The religious community acts as sent for and by Christ; it has an eschatological role no secular agency can approach. But at the same time the religious community must be a place of dialogue between the world and Christ—real physical, cultural, and intellectual contact. If the world kindly informs us that it no longer needs apostolates it once needed, we must drop them. If the world does need someone to raise a new voice for man, we must learn from the world of its needs.

Just as the horizon of American life, a secular and socio-technical life, determines the change in communal aspects of religious life, so the upheaval in the traditional structures of American life—in city, in school, in family—acts as catalyst for the re-evaluation and creative innovation in what should be the ministry of a Christian community. This carries forward the program we outlined at the beginning. Our program reverses the procedure of renewal beginning with law and ending with personnel. Radicalism begins with persons and their world, with the psychologically developed ability to change and with the critical view of what is happening in the world. It begins with ourselves and our communities, as men and women, and as Christians from, within, and to the world. It goes on to "filter" this through the perspectives of the life and gospel of Jesus. It concludes with the law being the enabler of freedom and with a synthesis of policy, programs, institutions, structures, and persons.

THE THEOLOGY OF REVOLUTION

The contemporary theological problematic which corresponds to the apostolate is the theology of social change. Some call it the theology of revolution. There is revolution all around us. There is a revolution by which, through technology, the mass-media, and the fear of world destruction, the world is becoming one. There is the same dissatisfaction among students in New York, Paris, Prague, Lima, dissatisfaction with the lack of creative optimism in present politicians. (We recall the motto of the French students: *"imagination au pouvoir*—imagination reaching for power."*) There is a revolution of the emerging third world, and the discovery of the seeds of self-destruction in poverty and racism in America. There is the generation gap, the breakdown in communications between groups, and more important, the fact that poor American Negroes no longer want to be like the middle-class whites just as the new African capitals do . not want to ape London. They want something better, and as the late Robert Kennedy said, they dream about what could be rather than accept what is. John Gardner has said: "Man is in trouble. And if you are not filled with foreboding you don't understand your time. The times cry out for swift and effective institutional change to avert disaster. But our institutions resist change with unholy stubbornness."[1]

[1] Remarks to the Democratic Convention's Platform Committee, August 1968.

Social change for the Christian is positive because of the goodness of God, because of the power he has given to man over creation, because of the ultimately positive course of history through the presence of God's image and grace and Son in the world. Revolution is realistic because it takes seriously—as present now and in the future—evil as a state and sin as personal failing. Revolution viewed from the aspect of sin is feared because it may be violent, and violence, like every evil, tends to lead to greater evil. Yet, no social change for the Christian is ultimately political; the Christian places the values of person and of the Christian gospel beyond the establishment of a new political order. Political structure is the milieu for human life, but it is not the eschaton itself, nor the Kingdom of God. At the same time, it is contrary to the Suffering Servant's resurrection to explain away suffering and exploitation by promising a heaven to those who live patiently in the midst of cruelty. The question of violence and non-violence is a serious one, but it is not yet crucial for American religious as they now live. The question is important, because there is a possibility that entire nations could substitute organized non-violence for military expenditures. It is, secondly, possible that large scale war might be able to be eliminated, and in its final stages of realization this movement would involve an emphatic "No!" to war through non-violent protest and civil disobedience. Often, however, the civil and religious establishment confuses non-violent protest with doing nothing at all. The active involvement of religious against the exploitation of minorities in race and income is absolutely necessary if this impression is to be corrected. Since Americans are result-oriented, sign and witness must include concrete action. American Christians, because of this orientation and because the Gospel itself has a "political" sphere, cannot avoid protest and demonstration against the American establishment's exploitation at home and abroad.

Richard Schaull, professor at Princeton and consultant for

the World Council of Churches, singles out certain aspects of the Judaeo-Christian biblical tradition which have implications for social change. God is the Creator and Ruler of all spheres of nature and society. God is viewed by the Bible as creating what is good. There is a strong eschatological emphasis leading toward a resolution for good. This goodness, development, and eschatology of the world culminates in the messianism of the Old and New Testaments. "In this atmosphere of revolution, the Messiah is the central figure. He arises after the house of David has been destroyed, as a shoot out of an apparently dead trunk. In Isaiah especially, central attention is given to his role as a political revolutionary, an emphasis that breaks forth in the New Testament in the Magnificat. In the life, death, and resurrection of Jesus, the messianic theme of destruction and restoration finds new meaning and focus."[2]

Biblical messianism is not an otherworldly elevation, but a dynamism within human growth.

The central biblical images, symbols, and stories focus attention not so much on the nature of man—a child of nature who also transcends it, created in the image of God and sinner—as upon man, the historical being, moving forward toward the goal of full humanization. The accent is on the new man, the new humanity as it is becoming reality in the concreteness of historical existence and in response to an initiative from beyond itself. The dominant theme is the movement from the first to the second Adam, from the first to the second advent. Jesus Christ is the new man who accompanies fallen humanity in his whole history, who in his resurrection instituted a new life, and who makes it possible for man to look forward to a greater fulfillment in the coming age.[3]

Messianism shows how concrete situations force new plans and new decisions to be made for a future. Messianism does not ac-

[2] Richard Shaull, "Revolutionary Change in Theological Perspective," in H. Cox, editor, *The Church Amid Revolution* (New York, 1967), pp. 31f.
[3] Richard Shaull, "Theology and the Transformation of Society," *Theology Today,* 25 (1968), p. 25.

cept the status quo or calm, slow, uncertain change as the only alternative. In the Bible God tears down at times in order to build up. "For those who are engaged in the revolutionary struggle, such a theological witness may be of no less importance. Their temptation is to give up in despair in the face of structures which seem totally resistant to change or resort to acts of desperation which only makes the situation worse. To them, the Christian symbols can suggest that crucifixion *is* victory over principalities and powers."[4] Not only has God created his world, he is involved in the very process of "creating" man and his world. The God who is tearing down old structures in order to create the conditions for a more human existence is himself in the midst of the struggle. The creative word is incarnate; the Spirit is sent. "God has taken human form in the concreteness of historical life and has called us to follow this path if we are to be the salt of the earth and the light of the world (Matt. 5:13–14)."[5] It is the Christian belief in the action of God, in a history of salvation, in a messianic and eschatological thrust which gives him the confidence to work for change, to be liberated from the structures. Yet, the revolutionary may not make an idol of change or revolution.

Jesus Christ enters into the progressive evolution of mankind.

The peculiar dynamic of this position is the result of the association of this hope for man with a particular historical person, Jesus of Nazareth, in whom we have a concrete indication of what such a new humanity can mean. Jesus, the Messiah—a political, in fact, a revolutionary figure—is the instrument of human emancipation. The Messiah has come in the past, yet still continues his work; thus, liberation is both an actuality and a possibility toward which we are moving.[6]

[4] *Ibid.,* pp. 28f.
[5] Shaull, "Revolutionary Change," p. 39.
1966), p. 228.
[6] Richard Shaull, Carl Oglesby, *Containment and Change* (New York,

APOSTOLATE AND REVOLUTION

Jesus Christ as incarnate and risen is the promise that even the historical and revolutionary process, which will in this world have many set-backs, will reach a positive resolution. At the same time the value of each individual is such that the eschaton will give his life permanent meaning and reality. There is, then, a new creation, beginning now, one which is not an apocalyptic climax or tired end of history and revolution. What should Christians work for in order to help establish this new world? The Church must be free to be what it "is." The first step is not to revolt, but to be true to the freedom and radicalness in Jesus Christ. The Church and the Christian must be true to transcendence and transcend systems taken for granted, evils justified as inevitable. He must be loyal not to creation as we possess it, but to the Creator. What are the specifically Christian elements which we believe are at the center of God's humanizing activity in the world? One of these is forgiveness of past sin and freedom to begin again for a better future. Another is a variation of this, reconciliation between men and God, and between men and men—justice can be introduced.

Shaull writes of the new and unprecedented polarization between those who have enjoyed the benefits of the status quo and those who are most anxious to change it in every nation and on every level (including that of the student and that of the Catholic religious). Social revolution is the primary fact with which our generation will have to come to terms.[7]

If the analysis shown is correct, it will be on the frontiers of revolution that many of the major issues of humanization and dehumanization will be decided in our modern world; it will be on these frontiers that those most concerned for the well-being and for the future of man will find themselves involved. This will be true not only for those young people —from both the privileged and underprivileged classes—who discover that their responsibility for their fellowmen leads them to participation

[7] Shaull, "Revolutionary Change," p. 28.

101

in revolution, but it will also be true for those in positions of power in the established order who understand the world in which they are living and feel compelled to work for change. If we hope to preserve the most important elements of our cultural, moral, and religious heritage and to contribute to the shaping of the future, we cannot remain outside the revolutionary struggle or withdraw from it.[8]

Shaull goes on to describe a need in today's conflict. "This is what we most desperately need today: men liberated for creativity, participating in a community in which they are forced to die daily in order to create new ideas, new perspectives, new experiments, new institutions, new political possibilities."[9] Is there a better description of what religious communities should be?

Gospel and Crisis Situation

We need not agree that the Kingdom of God is identifiable with social change. Our first mission as apostles is the preaching of that Kingdom which has a past (the events of the life, death, and resurrection of Christ); a present (the worship of God in the liturgy and in the service of all men); and a future (the parousia of Christ, the resolution of the universe and humanity in God). Indeed, only Christianity is the real secularity and final social change, because only it promises the redemption of the concrete, the material, the secular, rather than its absorption or death.

Most people we encounter have heard of Christianity; the vast majority of Americans profess it. So our mission is to make

[8] *Ibid.*, p. 29. Eric Hoffer, commenting on the Negro revolution in the United States, writes: "Mass movements are often the means by which a population undergoing drastic change acquires a sense of rebirth and a new identity." *New York Times Magazine* (November 29, 1964), p. 109, cited in Shaull, *ibid.*, p. 28.

[9] Shaull, *Containment and Change*, p. 21.

more explicit what is often implicit. The worship of God in the liturgy has both scriptural word and eucharistic event; the secular worship of God in men has both word and action: the critical prophetic word of the Gospel and the effective service of men. Both have a direct relationship to social improvement. They urge it on, give it hope, but also criticize as to whether it has real value for men. What is the precise role of religious communities here? They are neither the entire People of God nor the local bishop with his presbytery. *One primary role* (and this does not exclude secondary directions) *of religious communities is to be the Christian presence in the crisis centers of human and social change.* By "presence" I mean neither pure social action nor withdrawn approval but Gospel-word and Gospel-action. This is not a local or economic direction but a theological one. There are many crisis situations; we have no lack of them. The most neglected Catholics may not be those in the slums but in the suburban parishes; the action is as much in Michigan or Illinois as in The Congo or South Africa. Regardless, does it not fall upon the religious to give the sacrifice, the personnel, the time, and the expertise to witness to Christ incarnate in the crisis areas of the Church and society? Our histories support this, for most if not all communities were founded for a particular crisis.

As we speak of personnel and effort being directed to these crises, we must also develop a creative awareness about them. We need to encourage the prophetic voices which point out where persecution, injustice, and despair are appearing. We need to think radically in terms of new apostolates. There are tremendous needs for ministry and Christian criticism in the penal systems, not simply supplying chaplains, but asking about the systems, its employees, its goals, and its often inhuman abuses. We need to have dedicated Christians who have the mobility and training to be of service where justice is abused. For every case which attracts attention to the totalitarian control of people, many escape notice. We need Christians who will risk being with the young, the addicted *on the streets,* and not just in nearly empty church basements. We need support for South American missionaries who are amazed by and aware of the dangers of exploitation by American business enterprises there. We need, again, to risk new life-styles and approaches to the complex, pluralistic world of the university. We need great numbers of sisters in religious education, in dope addiction work (rather than in the administration of hospitals). Naturally these ministries imply in their very conception risk and failure. But the religious life must decide in favor of risk, for that is how the decision for life presents itself today.

My joining of the theology of social change and revolution with the apostolate of religious communities is not meant to be an inspiring metaphor or slogan. It implies for all religious a critical examination of any self-perpetuating machinery, of any system for prestige or profit. The needs of the times, people as they are—these measure the apostolate. And they have nothing to do with income level. Everyone rushing into poverty areas will not solve all our problems.

Revolutionary Origins

Most men and women who gathered groups of Christians around them did so to meet a particular need. This need was always connected to the Christian gospel, but it was not always the preaching or praying of that gospel itself. Hospitals, prisons, schools, libraries, universities were also seen as needs of a particular age. The history of these founders and foundresses is a litany of persecution and misunderstanding, showing how little the Church and society want to accept Christian revolutionaries. More revolutionary were the great breakthroughs in monastic and religious life: those of Benedict, Dominic and Francis, Ignatius Loyola, Charles de Foucauld. In their lives we see the risk and difficulty of developing a new form of religious life. How strongly the early Benedictines, those monks behind the *Rule,* had to fight for community against autocracy, for common sense against rigoristic asceticism. How unpopular was the literal following of the gospel of Francis. Nothing seemed less promising than the mobility, higher education, and freedom which Dominic had in mind. Ignatius' ideas were put into practice in a most turbulent world, with empire, medieval order, churches collapsing and emerging around him. What is striking about these breakthroughs is their close relationship to what was happening in the world, and their bond with the non-clerical life. Benedictines were communities of Christians, not of clerics; Francis' conception was similar to that of many bands of lay-preachers beginning to appear in the twelfth century. They would be groups of poor Christians practicing and preaching the gospel, freed from the entanglements of the great medieval Church.[10] Did Dominic retain the clerical aspect mainly because it was the road to education? There are many aspects of the early life of the friars which show a strong re-affirmation of the lay over the clerical. These are simply a sign of the role of the world in the origins of religious life: the dialogue of stimulus and response.

A central revolutionary mission in religious communities is their role as critical renewers of the Church, and as missionaries to the needs of the wold. Unlike the Protestant sectarian communities, the Catholic congregations and orders live in a constant tension with the world they wish to serve and even with the ecclesiastical establishment which finds them threatening. To

[10] See M.-D. Chenu, "Monks, Canons, and Laymen in Search of the Apostolic Life," *Nature, Man and Society in the Twelfth Century* (Chicago, 1968), pp. 202ff.

what extent is criticism of the establishment at the very heart of religious life? Some theologians suggest that the orders must rediscover this again for the benefit of our time when criticism of institutions (which preserve themselves with an "unholy stubbornness") is so necessary. How can we discover, without making impossible and sensationalistic demands, the revolutionary character of each community? This is deeply related to the religious life as a life of a certain intensity and a full-time, professional Christian apostolate. Every religious community should be self-critical, that is, it should periodically ask what is its *real* contribution to the urban, suburban, or rural community in which it lives. Is it simply keeping wheels going? The community should prepare itself in prayer and community life for possible criticism, and for more strenuous tests ahead. There should be a sense of personal sharing between communities, so that those in greater need, deeper in the crisis-situations of contemporary American life have greater resources and support to draw on. Some percentage of every community's income and effort should be devoted to the alleviation of ignorance, poverty, and injustice. That means that every community should be actively involved—at least part-time—in what can be honestly called crises. In the past a few communities have done this in a rather schizoid way, moving one day a week from suburbia to ghetto. Perhaps a better plan would be to see how the suburb itself could be involved in the ghetto; this would be more effective . . . and more dangerous.

Each community through discussion must work out its own theology and life of secular and revolutionary theology. This cannot be done by reading books or bringing in lecturers. It comes from experience and from encounter with the characteristics and signs of our times, from reflections upon this experience in the light of the gospel, and from sharing insights with each other. This development of an individual theology, liturgy and prayer-life for a particular community is essential.

106

Conclusion

The issue is the Incarnation but from a particular point of view. The first heresy denied that Jesus the Christ was a man. Early writings tell us of the Apostle John's abhorrence of Cerinthus who taught that Jesus was a phantom. The greatest challenge to faith is believing that the Logos became flesh and blood.

The issue is Christ, but Christ in his incarnational identification with each man and woman. The conflict is over the Mystical Body of Christ. If St. Paul had not said it, we might hesitate to speak of continuing the Incarnation in each of us, of the Mystical Body of Christ (which McLuhan says has an unprecedented opportunity to take shape in the tuned-on electronic era). Now the challenge is to affirm by concrete action that Jesus Christ identifies—is identifying right now—himself with each person. "Which of these three do you think proved himself a neighbor to the man who fell into the brigands' hands?" (Luke 10:37). "I tell you solemnly, in so far as you did this to one of these least of these brothers of mine, you did it to me" (Matt. 25:40). It is difficult to accept the awesome implications of the Mystical Body of Christ amidst the increasing unity of the global village and the revolution of minority protest. The ultimate question for religious life is whether it can come into existence out of the throbbing currents of life today, whether it can bring together—incarnate—the Spirit and creation. Joan Baez concludes her autobiography with these thoughts:

A friend of mine told me it would be risky to write about Jesus. I'll risk it. I wonder if Jesus knows what's happening on earth these days. Don't bother coming around, Jesus.

Jesus, gold and silver—standing naked in a roomful of modern men. What nerve. Jesus, gold and silver—you have no boots on, and you have no helmet or gun—no briefcase. Powerful Jesus, gold and silver with young, thousand-year-old eyes. You look around and you know

107

you must have failed somewhere. Because here we are, waiting on the eve of destruction with all the odds against any of us living to see the sun rise one day soon.

> You, Dear Reader—
> You are Amazing Grace,
> You are a Precious Jewel.

Only you and I can help the sun rise each coming morning. If we don't, it may drench itself out in sorrow.[11]

---

[11] Joan Baez, *Daybreak* (New York, 1968), p. 191.

6. Structural Radicalism

Institutions are important because they control people. Human behavior matures or stifles in different environments, and our environments are to a great extent the product of institutions, structures, buildings, and social patterns. Jesus Christ saw that he could not introduce a new law, a new creation, a new kind of relationship between God and man as long as the religious institutions of the world controlled man's life improperly. As important as faith and Spirit may be, even they can be frustrated by impotent or ossified institutions. Community life is particularly subject to institutional control, and Christians have been for some time hesitant to see institutions as changeable and subservient to their lives. Like the gospel, we must presuppose an openness to structural criticism, renewal, or replacement.

THE END OF AUTHORITY?

What does it mean to speak of radicalism in structure? Instead of beginning with authority or people in authority, we begin with our own community. One of the structures helping or hurting what people do and how they live is community. We belong to many different communities: a community of friends, a local and larger religious community, a city, county, state, and national community. Man has taken for granted in the past that authority had groups of people to employ or control. Authority is not ultimate but ministerial; this is being recognized everywhere, but it is part of Jesus' religious revolution. It is important today to reverse the whole relationship of authority and community. We have to start thinking from another point of view. Just as renewal has not been sufficient for the deeper issues of religious life from a radical point of view, so we can use a phrase which indicates the crisis in authority. *We are at the period in history where there is an end to authority.* Part of what is happening in society and in the Church, and in religious life, is an indication that an end is coming to authority. Obviously that doesn't mean that religious are all going to become anarchists, hippies, or Quakers. In fact, a new view will describe an almost intolerable office for those people in authority. When we look at society, we see an end of authority, if by authority we mean certain types of authoritative control. Conflicts in our society question authority. Students want to know why they should be put on computer cards and shuffled through four years of requirements. Why do we have elections, but no choices? Why are lakes polluted by businesses? The war in Vietnam will come to an end; why are people dying there each week? Behind these questions are lonely, threatened, and obsolete models of authority.

This kind of questioning is not a denial of all authority, but a critique of the exercise of authority. It rejects some kinds of authority not because they guide, direct, and organize but precisely because they do *not.* Authority is demythologized, encouraged to mature along with the rest of society. When it refuses these initially friendly gestures, it is mocked or rejected, to the detriment of both sides. From this point of view, there is not a crisis of authority in either Church or society, but a crisis of the exercise of authority.

The authority that is coming to an end is the authority that tried to do everything. This authority is dying because it has been diminishing for centuries. Declining authority has had three characteristics. First of all, it has made most of the decisions. To say "most" of the decisions is to say "all" of the decisions. Renewal and political liberalism would be a process by which the person who made *all* of the decisions now makes *most* of the decisions. But this change is insufficient in the present crisis. Secondly, authority makes decisions *alone*. Modifiers such as "in consultation with" were always escape clauses. How much effort has been spent in ecclesiastical law to protect authority from being bound by the opinions of others? Now we are in a situation where many need to be bound by the created ideas of others. Thirdly, there was a theological-social theory of divine assistance. The divine will was channeled into a few persons. Criticizing politically had the moral overtones of *possibly* challenging God.

Why is this kind of authority disappearing? Because we live with people who are educated, technologically advanced, and increasingly secular. People want to work out their own destinies. We have people in society and in the churches who can get us out of our crises. As long as we refuse to listen to them we are not going to find solutions from God in prayer. We do not need people to make "most" of the decisions or to make them alone. Aristotle and Thomas Aquinas point out that we have people in authority because they are able to do something for us. The goal is to have intelligent people with leadership deftly drawing on ideas in order to enable human life rather than tradition and order. Widespread education necessarily reduces the role of authority. As education inceases, political authority decreases. When you have a certain percentage of people educated, you can have democracy. Perhaps that is why young people are vocal today. Is increased improvement in American education precisely responsible for students wanting to burn down administration buildings?[1] Similarly, the layman who initiates a floating parish is not attacking Church authority; rather, he takes Vatican

[1] See P. C. Rooney, "Educational Processes and Theology," *Projections: Shaping an American Theology for the Future* (New York, 1970).

II's theology seriously. Also important here is change. If things are going to keep on changing, lonely authority becomes an impossible task. Constant mobility demands that the group makes more decisions. Authority, blind to the complexity of life and grace and wanting to make most or all of the decisions alone aided by "divine" help, is rendered incredible.

OBEDIENCE AS POSITIVE COMMITMENT

What does authority coming to an end mean for radicalism in community structure? Before we discuss this, let us reject the spirituality claiming obedience is blind or central to religious life. Many were taught that to remain obedient is to suffer, that it is a great virtue to have yourself moved and changed from job to job and plainly suffer. This is unchristian, stoic. Commitment to a Christian community at work is the purpose of obedience, not ascetic discipline or martyrdom.

Obedience as worthwhile martyrdom is rare. There is no purpose in justifying wrong decisions about other people as martyrdom. Obedience is not the goal of the spiritual life, nor of community life. Responsibility, harmony, and efficiency are goals of community. Every handbook says that the goal of religious life and the spiritual life is charity, charity within the community and effective ministry to the Church. Authority rests with God who is ineffable and transcendent. It is blasphemous to speak as if God is indentifiable in all the details of life. This is contrary to a sound theology of creation of men as free and responsible agents within the milieu of grace.[2]

This does not mean that office, that lasting position of leadership and coordination, does not exist any longer among re-

---

[2] "Man is the master of his acts [although] ultimately man's free will is moved by some principle above the human mind, namely, by God." Thomas Aquinas, *Summa Theologiae*, I–II, q. 109, a. 2, 1.

ligious, nor that authority is at the constant whim of the community. The community where authority is daily questioned is no community but a collection of hesitant and uncertain people. Authority exists to bring to focus the community. The ceremony of pronouncing vows in public to a particular sister, priest, or brother is not a medieval anachronism, but a liturgical and symbolic act within the community, for the person who receives the vows does so as representative of the community, the community in its broader dimensions. What are these dimensions? Continuity, eschatological expectation, dialogue within the Mystical Body of Christ present throughout space and time among men are a few. The community which has nothing lasting or continuous about it is not worth a lifetime commitment. So it is not enough to say that authority in religious life is never more than the will, impact, or commitment of a local community at that moment—any more than it is correct to see authority in terms of a "father," a "master," a "general," or a "mother" with a large family (of children!). It is precisely because authority must bridge the gap between this particular group and the broader lines of the secular (for instance, history) and the sacred (the mystery of faith *in* the religious life) that it is difficult to describe. It can never be described adequately through laws.

POLITICAL REVERSALS

What kind of radicalism are we looking for in community structure?

First of all, we have to reverse the entire political structure of the religious life by turning it upside down. There will be a series of reversals. Grace will be seen more in terms of functions and charisms, and openness to charisms and missions than in terms of states and habits to be guarded. The local unit will be

113

primary rather than the province or the congregation. The model for religious life will not be the novitiate but various local communities, which themselves are open to cycles of change. Decisions and commands will yield to consensus. Authority will emerge as leadership and service. Life will not be something to be escaped or controlled, but an intangible vitality to be served and incarnated.

The unity and starting point for religious life becomes the local community. Previously the basic unit was the motherhouse, even the novitiate. The novitiate became the ideal place of religious life. After the novitiate everything went downhill. We have to reverse the process, and make the basic unit of religious life the local community. If we study the history of religious life, we see that this has been the case when religious life has flourished. The local community attracts vocations. Today people are more and more in the horizontal dimension; they identify with people. The local community is where life and vocation will or will not exist. Yet, at the same time that the pyramid of religious life is turned upside down, leadership and direction must still permeate and give direction. The pyramid is not only reversed, it is set in motion; the local community cannot provide all of the motion alone; as we will see, that is where authority-as-practical-service enters.

Secondly, in management and development the individual person has value. Religious life must exist in each person committed to this way of life. To begin with the local community has dangerous implications. It means in this time of transition (if not always) the local communities will reflect pluralism. There will have to be different kinds of local communities, simply because the local community has and lives in a pluralism of legitimate options. A community finds out what is going on in a certain area and develops a corresponding apostolate. This cannot be exactly the same as another a thousand miles away. You cannot have local communities in Albuquerque, Chicago, and Quito living exactly the same way. You cannot have local communities in grade schools and colleges which live and pray identically. Secondly, in a transition period it is not right to ask everyone in a wide spectrum of renewal and radicalism to live exactly the same way. It is unjust to older sisters to ask them to go through a "factory" where they are "renewed," and it is unjust to younger sisters to ask them to live in a hesitant way, which is not meaningful or creative of new models of religious life. As long as the problem surrounding pluralism is not solved, we will not have religious life. We will have a conflict of people who are trying to find out what religious life is, but who do not know. This will not encourage young people to enter, since no clear image of religious life is available.

If the primacy of the local community implies pluralism, ultimate value of the individual person involves sound community and questions autocratic authority. It is a basic principle of evangelical Christianity that the individual person is *the* unit. Jesus excoriates Jewish religion and the Pharisees for using tricks to avoid paying respect to the individual person and to God. The individual person is so elevated in the twenty-fifth chapter of Matthew that when Christ comes as the eschatological judge he identifies himself with the miserable of the earth as his criterion for judgment. For whom does religious life exist? Does it exist for the laity? For the bishops? For the Pope? Does it exist for a General in Rome? Does it exist for buildings and structures? Or, does it exist for the people who are in it? Religious life does not even exist ultimately for the salvation of others, but for the personal Christian development of those entering it. To take Christian maturity and the development of the individual seriously would cause a revolution in the world—and that is radicalism. To say that religious life centers around the people in it helps counter a credibility gap about Christian love. People see no sense for a person to commit himself to evangelical ideals and then to be caught up in a whirl-wind of something over

115

which they have no control, something boring, meaningless, and routine. The goal or claim is too great for the reality. This does not advocate that everybody go off and "do their own thing." That is not possible, but why project these extremes right away to contradict the principle? We do not know what will happen, but we must start placing people first. A person's life as a Christian and his or her ministry has the primacy. This involves setting up priorities, priorities in institutions and in Christian communal life. Putting person and community first is difficult, but the Holy Spirit is more likely to be with us if we give priority to these scriptural values. What should the community put first? What can the community and congregation undertake? A first consideration in priorities is the people involved. There cannot be a policy or goal in religious life such as running six or sixty schools. Religious communities exist to serve in the concrete, but they must consider numbers and buildings in the abstract. Today all must learn to practice humility and detachment not only on a personal level but on an institutional one.

It is important to build into the religious life, as into all other human societies, structures of two-way communications and of feedback. Personnel and grievance boards are necessities, particularly because of the great abuses of the past and because of the remaining distrust of provincial or congregational "establishment." Recently CBS news commentators pointed out that we are in the midst of the third presidential term where poor communications interrupt the flow between chief executive and the American people. Evidently, then, good communications are not easy. This is complicated by the fact that the religious life is the inseparable union of Christian life-style and community with effective apostolate. There must be ways of feeding back the pulse of a community to its members, and this at the level of life and personal fulfillment as well as professional effectiveness. Feedback in these dimensions is difficult and can hardly be developed without patience, redevelopment of spiritual and psychological attitudes, and professional help.

At this point we mention the value of seeking professional help from management consultants in the rethinking of administrative and decision-making structures. The behavioral and social sciences have developed laws and models of how institutions and groups should be organized in order to function well, to function humanly at the group and personal levels. There are ways of arranging staff and administrators, of weaving together policy, program, structure, and personnel, and there are injurious arrangements to avoid. "Authority" is not a profound Christian theological problem; it has been imprecisely raised to this level by men. Authority and administration are utilitarian, pragmatic services, and their efficient development is neither a matter of frequent divine inspiration nor grass-roots experimentation, but the concern of sciences. Various crises in structural reorganization need professional critique and guidelines.

AUTHORITY AS LEADERSHIP AND COORDINATION

What will happen to authority? For lack of a better word we might call that which should emerge from the old authority *leadership*. Leadership differs from authority. Authority controls; leadership guides and inspires. Almost anyone can govern according to law and force. To do so demands no positive qualities in the laws or in the enforcers of the laws. Leaders, however, are difficult to find, to create. Leadership demands persons with ideas who can coordinate and communicate what is going on in the community.

There is a new model for authority in the religious life: *the pastoral center of coordination*. What does such a pastoral center do? It coordinates and communicates what is going on in

117

communities. It feeds information, personnel, development, ideas to the people it serves. There are many relationships here. For instance, teachers need lines to other teachers, to grants, and opportunities for education; there must be communication within the wider groupings of communities, with the diocese. Such a center functions at the level of life, education, and apostolate, enabling help and information and support to flow between each local community and a hundred other places. Doesn't this approach make sense in terms of American society? We are no longer a society needing people to tell us what to do, but we are precisely a society in which the information explosion and the rise of competency staggers the imagination. We desperately need people to tell us *what* to do: not what *to do,* but *what* can be done—especially on the level of competency in apostolates.

In this arrangement authority itself would become an apostolate. The people involved in leadership at the provincial, congregational, and international levels would themselves be a pastoral team. They would live together, but travel a great deal. They would truly be serving all the others by leading and aiding.

Their authority would also involve "spiritual" leadership. Again, this would not be as in the past when the provincial came to frown at the level of local observance. Authority still has a mission of spiritual leadership at this level, but now a more difficult one. It is not that of interior spiritual direction—but rather of representing the cutting edge of the gospel. The local community is not going to become suddenly the kingdom of God on earth. Tense conflicts may multiply. Leadership comes as the critical edge and voice of the New Testament, not armed with law and an horarium, but with a critical view of the world and with the gospel. It asks how the local community is actually living before the sign of the New Testament. Is this community depending on an establishment? Is it free? Is it emotionally capable of being human? Is it sharing with other needy communities? How is it seen by world and Church, by the young and the poor? Here again difficult questions are asked. The need for authority in religious life, as in the Church, remains. It becomes the voice—through the reversal of pastoral service—of communication, growth, and the gospel. Now both authority and individual are free in a "world come of age" (Bonhoeffer) to follow Thomas Aquinas's description of the New Law of Jesus Christ: "the grace of the Holy Spirit manifest in faith operative through love."[3]

[3] Thomas Aquinas, *Summa Theologiae*, I–II, q. 108, a. 1.

7. Christian Radicalism

The processes which play such a prominent role in developments within society and Church, the catalysts for change in religious life, are also at the root of the profound uncertainty in Christians' attitudes toward prayer, toward what has been called the "interior" or "spiritual" life. Religious quests are going on all around us, and although there has perhaps never been a time or a people so caught up in ultimate questions and in struggles to break out of the dehumanizing and material, still we have not yet found a living God to respond to this. It is, of course, part of the struggle to be critical, skeptical or belligerent toward past gods. Our religious quest tries psychedelic drugs as doors to religious experience and researches a new morality to find a place for freedom, honesty, and love. It encompasses Protestants, who find it so contrary to the spirit of the times to believe that man who explores the moon and surrounds himself with music could be "totally corrupt." It demands a new maturity for Catholics who find the once sacred rubrics and static moral imperatives of their Church extensively changed and radically challenged in only five years.

Secularization could not but have an effect upon the Christian's attitude toward his personal life as a believer. Secularization is all-encompassing as the horizon of American life today. We have already mentioned that its attitude toward religion is ambiguous, including two forces. The one (seemingly anti-religious) assumes that the secular, the non-religious, is the ordinary milieu and horizon of life. The other liberates religion from idolatrous relationships to things, rules, laws, and can reveal an openness to the "holy." The secular does not exclude faith or mature religion, but in its process of establishing the inner network of relationships in man's world, it rejects superstition, idolatory, and magic (the divinizing of human laws, rubrics, things, and actions), and at the same time is open to the individual's personal and communal search for the disclosure of the godly and the human in life itself.

Secularization affects prayer. In the midst of greater and greater technological progress by man, the severe, unsettling question arises as to whether prayer can be effective, when the computer and rocket are not. Is anyone listening at all? Secondly, it becomes increasingly difficult to live in two worlds: the work-a-day world and an "interior" or "religious" world. This latter may be in one's own mind or in a church decked out with sacred people and pictures. But there is only one world, and Christianity is a "worldly" gospel. A faith which sees the world different than it is, a hope which finds satisfaction only in the next life, a charity which self-consciously asks about itself twice a day without seeing any transformation in the world around it—these once credible dynamics of the interior life are rejected. The sacraments are rediscovered as human, joyful liturgy. They are not the domain of rubricians but experiences which are free and open to different kinds of realization. Magic is excluded from the liturgy, and from the decisions of ecclesiastical superiors. The age-old mystery of God's transcendence and involvement has been recovered. This mystery is solved fully only by the Incarnation.

Revolution and social change also demythologize and threaten the "spiritual life." They say Christian life cannot be merely a "spiritual" one. By focusing our attention mercilessly on the needs of our neighbor, they do not allow us to cultivate a leisurely and introspective interior life. They make us recall that faith, hope, love, prayer, humility cannot exist only interiorly.

121

Any division between the interior religious life and its exterior living is consistently forbidden by Jesus in his struggle with the Jewish religious establishment. Faith, hope, love, the beatitudes, and the Kingdom are politico-theological concepts, involving us in the political sphere of life. Jesus was executed for both political and religious reasons. Social change reduces the evil of credibility gaps and the evil of separating Christianity into inner and outer worlds. It throws us into greater contact with the world around us, with suffering and rejoicing humanity. As in a multi-media presentation, we are bombarded with the hopes and the sorrows of men. At the same time God withdraws, because he is not someone above the clouds, not someone rather ineptly mixing in human affairs with a rare miracle and an inept and weak providence. But, if God is not someone keeping the world and its turmoil from completely boiling over, where is he, what is he, who is he . . . and what does he mean to me? God is absent. That is the crisis of Christian piety, of the spiritual life, of being-a-Christian today.

THE ABSENCE OF GOD

Henri de Lubac has said, "Everytime man gives up a particular way of thinking, he fears he is losing God."[1] We may experience this loss personally through our inability to pray or in the increasing lack of meaning of a phrase like "all-provident." We may feel an increased, almost unbridgeable distance between ourselves and God, between ourselves and others. The dying God-is-dead-theology was a sign of changing times; it pointed to the growing questioning of religious traditions and presuppositions. Behind this questioning are deeper but allied unrests: social concern, potential for protest, the conscious or subliminal

[1] Cited in J. B. Metz, "Gott vor uns," *Ernst Bloch zu ehren* (Frankfurt, 1964), p. 233.

122

influence of television and technology. A child no longer looks with religious awe at a star-filled sky but asks with pride: "Which one of those is ours?" E. Schillebeeckx writes:

Our situation requires us to speak of God in a way quite different from the way in which we have spoken of him in the past. If we fail to do this, we ourselves shall perhaps still be able to experience God in outmoded forms, but clearly our own witness of and discussion of God will be met by most people with headshaking disbelief as mumbojumbo. It is partly because we are blind to the "signs of the times" that God's word, in all that we say of him, is returning to him void.[2]

And yet, today's American society—young and old—represents a remarkable level of religious concern. Innumerable explicit and implicit religious quests are depicted by films, TV, folk-rock; yet America encounters only more and more difficulty searching for the real God. At the center of this concern is a disturbing storm-center. It may prove to be what is sought, for God may be at the turbulent eye of this quest.

There are two extremes in the problem of prayer to God. Both are tempting, but both are to be avoided as humanly and theologically immature. The first is to say that of those who question, doubt, or find God absent most or all are perverse, proud, malicious or blind. Herbert Richardson points out in *Toward An American Theology* that there are different kinds of "atheism" and religious uncertainty.[3] There is not just atheism born of intellectual study or of ecclesiastical scandal—situations which at the very deepest level of the emotions and mind block out the presence of God. There are other "atheisms": the atheism of boredom before preachers and churches who have "thingified" God, who have drawn him not out of the vitality of life and the gospel but have imprisoned him in rituals and administrative red tape. There is an atheism of concern which respects

[2] *God the Future of Man* (New York, 1968), p. 53.
[3] New York, 1967.

God so much that it desires to liberate him from oppressive structures—linguistic and ecclesiastical—which make God appear
antiquated, slightly passé, ridiculous, incredible, cold.

The second possible reaction to our uncertain relationship to
God is to proclaim a theology which is so slick or "liberated"
that God's demise can be integrally accepted. The phrase "God
is dead" is literally unverifiable, mythical, and meaningless.
What is significant about extreme solutions is not that they are
false or short-lived, but that they are the easy solutions. Yet,
the problem—the problem beneath our relationship to God:
difficulty with prayer, searching unbelief—remains and grows.
The death of God was already announced in Western thought
almost a century ago by Nietzsche. Paul Tillich, Rudolf Bultmann, Karl Rahner are not theologians who fail to carry their
theology of God to a logical negative conclusion. Rather they are
the first generation trying to understand what Nietzsche meant.
The death of God as described by Nietzsche and interpreted by
Heidegger is not the death of a truly divine God, but the death
of a god imprisoned within political and religious structures,
within the inhumanity of man toward man. He would be a god
who justifies oppression and superstition and cheap salvation.
The "crazy man" (a nineteenth-century hippie?) who proclaimed the death of God in *Thus Spake Zarathustra* (whose
musical setting by Richard Strauss begins the film *2001*) was
actually on a quest for God but the bystanders could not help
him. Their god, he saw, was dying and deadly, and so he announced as an act of freedom that God was dead.

God is not dead, but he is absent. We sense the absence of a
dimension, of the response to a fundamental quest in all of us.
God is not here or he is rarely accessible. We are alone and
prayer is difficult. The subconscious supports of a super-world
or of a constant providence fade. Man dominates his growing
and waiting world, and simultaneously his misery in unwanted
wars and ghettoes and his hope in the accelerating race forward

124

grows. But God has withdrawn. Martin Heidegger writes: "The religious [dimension] will never be destroyed by logic, but rather through the fact that God withdraws himself."[4] Ingmar Bergman has referred to the theme of "The Silence" as "the silence of God."[5] Paul VI said recently, "God is silent, contemporary literature says. But he is silent to our natural ear in order to have us search for him and listen by other means."

Where to Go?

Naturally, "absence" or "withdrawal" must lose any local overtones. God does not ab-sent himself. As Creator and Trinity he is constantly sending himself. The change is on our part. Our distance-relationship to the transcendent changes according to the cultural, social, and theological atmosphere in which we live. We are rediscovering that God is godly, that he is Mystery, that he is Spirit, that as Jesus of Nazareth he overcame the horizontal-vertical problematic. But how does that help us who feel alone, who doubt that God is listening to us or particularly provident of us, who feel that our own satellites and communications systems block out or render silly our attempts to communicate with . . . God? Let us try to see further in precise terms of schools of spirituality why the old approaches are unrewarding, and ask if some recent figures in public and Christian life can give us hints of new directions in thinking and living as Christians. But first, we must pursue the absence of God. God is absent, and still we wish to find that Person who creates and leaves every person restless with a desire to reach beyond his or her humanity. Where shall we go? There are two possibilities. They are age-old ones, mutually inclusive, the dynamic components of the gospel of Incarnation: *the dimension of faith;*

[4] Martin Heidegger, *What Is Thinking?* (New York, 1968), p. 10.
[5] W. Hamilton, "The Silence of God," *Motive,* November 1966, p. 10.

the dimension of other people. The gospel indicates that here and here only can God be found. A too great "presence" of a god renders faith and community unnecessary; idolatory and power over the sacred leads to superstition and isolation. God's absence recalls his deeper, godly presence, accessible through a deeper faith, and through a mature and realistic love for those into whose lives we enter.

FAITH

Many developments in the present rapid evolution of religious life point to the need for a deeper faith. Faith must withstand the uncertainties of social change; it must find God without the help of ecclesiastical power, of clothes and institutions which bring privilege. Yet, often sisters and priests seem to be trying to replace faith, to replace it with renewal. If only the structures of religious life are changed enough, if only the old is fully replaced by the new, if only freedom is everywhere, then Utopia will be reached. Personal experience tells us that a too "practical" attitude toward renewal can terminate with religious losing all interest in their vocation. Faith can be the motivation for renewal, for honesty and improvement, but it cannot be replaced by them. The "secularization" of religious life, the response to radical problems and revolutionary apostolates need not a lighter faith but a deeper one, because faith now must stand very much alone and challenged in the midst of a changing world. Christ was without distinctive garb, without protective cloister, without power or privilege, but he knew the ambiguity of being in the world and yet not being of the world. He also knew that the presence, creation, and coming of the Kingdom was the work of faith, faith not as an internal life but as a creative power to change toward life in the face of evil and death. The absence of God, then, calls us to a deeper faith, one which can survive

126

the radical newness and challenging presence of Christian apostolic communities in the world.

To seek God alone in a deeper faith is difficult, for God remains absent. *The absence of God is, however, the presence of his Spirit.* The Spirit is present in the dynamics and enterprise of mankind. He is present in our drive toward the future, in the potential humanizing effect of technology, in the possibilities of raising all men to mature levels in education, science, art, politics. The Spirit is present as mankind attains the first glimpse of the possibility of peace and a truly human life for all. Yet the Spirit is also present interpreting the failures and the sins, the weakness and selfishness of man who does not struggle away from ambition to ministry. Our age is horizontally oriented; it is anthropocentric, personalistic, and pragmatically active. This is hardly something to be ashamed of, nor can it be changed. It is the mentality of the age. Christian faith can build upon it; it cannot replace it. Still these very characteristics are gifts of the Holy Spirit, and many of them are more evangelical than the keynotes of our immediate past. Clearly, Christians must plunge into the great movements of our age. This is what Bonhoeffer saw as the work of the mature Christian. This is what Hammarskjöld means by his remark: "In our era, the road to holiness necessarily passes through the world of action."[6] Our asceticism is attending meetings; our detachment is to allow old institutions to be replaced by uncertain new ones; our fortitude is to survive rapid and constant change; our blessing is to be able to work significantly for the option of a Kingdom of God.

PERSONS

To be person-oriented, to follow the Spirit does not imply merely work. The second path for pursuing the absence of God is not

[6] Dag Hammarskjöld, *Markings* (New York, 1965), p. xxi.

through work, but through persons. Action-orientation places Christians in the midst of people. The religious life as communal apostolate is eminently personal, for the dedicated Christian's life oscillates between persons in community and persons in the wider community of the world. The importance of persons lies behind the great desire in religious life to find meaningful community, to develop honest relationships between individuals. Religious life can no longer survive on a vague "charity," because the pressures of loneliness and meaninglessness—stimulated by social change and the absence of God—are too great. We are describing here a truly vast conflict, one which will determine the life or death of religious life. The pressures of secularization, of social change, the attraction of defending oneself from technological impersonalism through marriage (or through sex without marriage)—these are so strong that the religious life can survive only if it establishes for each community a social and personal life which finds self, others, and God in other men and women.

Each man and woman is an individual with unique talents and experiences, but each is also a member of various communities living and working with other people. We need to communicate with others about many things and at various levels. But, an enormous number of obstacles (many if not most unperceived) arise in communication. Human communication exists on several levels. One level is that of ideas. Our previous training and our background help us to feel comfortable in discussing things on an idea level. This is an important level. At the same time, another level of communication is present and in operation: the level of our feelings. Our feelings are an important part of our lives and must be reckoned with in our desire to communicate with others and if we are to communicate with others.

To communicate at the level of our feelings is not easy, for we are all inclined to be defensive and protective of ourselves. When we talk about the ideas of others and find ourselves attacked, we can always say that it was someone else's ideas. When we talk about how we feel about something or how we see something, we place ourselves at the center of criticism and disagreement. To help people be open to their feelings and to experiment with expressing these feelings is the purpose of *group dynamics* under professional direction. Methods of group dynamics are directed to helping people become more aware of their feelings and the feelings of others. An important discovery is that people in a group are individuals and react in different ways. Some people are inclined to talk about ideas, while others are oriented toward how they feel. During the course of the group, it is hoped that individuals will grow more comfortable with themselves and with the others in the group. There is the fear that when we are honest about our feelings, we will be standing alone. What we learn in group-processes is that others have the same feelings and the same experiences. Finding others who stand with us, so to speak, gives us strength to deal with our difficulties and rejoice in our successes.

One reason for interest in methods of group dynamics is that we are involved in creating community. Community does not emerge out of the air but requires the members to expend energy and effort. Community requires that people communicate with one another. If the community is to be significant, there must be significant communication between the members, communication which takes into consideration the deepest levels of the people involved. Group dynamics can be a painful process. An individual seeks to become aware of his feelings and the feelings of others. For some people this is a new experience and it does not come easily. Perhaps, group dynamics is not for everyone. Yet, it can be used profitably by and for religious as a foundation for the more honest and sensitive communities which must come.

129

COLLAPSE OF THE "SPIRITUAL LIFE"

Christian radicalism means radical thinking about living as a Christian today. This includes many levels of relationships: to God, to self, to other men as individuals, to a variety of communities. This chapter is discussing a phenomenon wider than religious life. All men feel the absence of God as our philosophers and our theater testify. So the following discussion of the future directions of the Christian life of prayer, faith, and service has been phrased in wider terms than the prayer-life of sisters or monks. Terms such as "spirituality" cannot be completely avoided. They are unfortunate because they imply a divorce, a separation between two worlds.

Very many religious can no longer bear to read five pages from the books which nourished their religious life for five to twenty-five years. Today's novice would find the former frameworks of spiritual theology meaningless if not ludicrous. This phenomenon of the collapse of much spiritual writing is made more severe by the fact that of all of fields of Christian reflection undergoing change since Vatican II, the least productive has been the spiritual life. To some extent this collapse of traditional spirituality can be explained by subtle but powerful shifts in thinking. Theology is shifting from being-orientation to person-orientation, and from state to action. These ideas have wide application and can explain what is happening in the Catholic Church's questioning of liturgy, institutions, priesthood, religious life, spirituality. For instance, we see that the priesthood is now better considered as a function of the community than as a state above the community; religious consecration is not a thing in itself without any need for justification, but is the power for preaching the gospel; the sign of religious persons and institutions is judged critically because sign finds its significative

130

value in action. This shift from being to person, from state to dynamism, may be helpful as an explanation but it, nonetheless, cannot make up for the collapse of much of the inspirational writings of the spiritual life. We remain in a vacuum. Still, we have the consolation that we have already entered this darkness, are probably at its rock-bottom, and can hope for some directions toward a new pluralistic meaning of being a Christian.

The Appeal of Pentecostalism

Not too long ago "Catholic Pentecostalism" appeared. There are many reasons for greeting this development of Catholic piety positively. It belongs to ecumenism not only to understand but to realize the positive aspects of other traditions in one's own ecclesial community. Pentecostalism means an openness to the Spirit, an informality of prayer, a sense of the Spirit's presence in vocation and in the living of that calling. Pentecostals parallel political and student movements by practicing openness to change and to the unthinkable—provinces of the Spirit. (We can pass over some of the less attractive and perhaps marginal characteristics of some Catholic Pentecostals: a bafflingly narrow and conservativistic theology, a closed or indifferent attitude toward our era of social change, a desperate quest for empirical manifestations in gifts of "religious tongues" and "healing." What is ironic is that these excesses are so manifestly contradictory to the writings of the Apostle of the Spirit, Paul.) The attraction of Pentecostalism is, I think, intimately connected with the collapse of so much traditional spirituality. Whether this attraction will last and be one of the new directions, whether it can be reconciled with the stronger action of the Spirit in society, whether the positive characteristics of spontaneity and personal prayer, of openness to the Spirit will be swallowed up

131

by theological reactionaries—all of this remains to be answered. What is important is to see the positive contributions such a movement makes at this time of crisis.

TOWARD NEW MENTORS

The absence of God is the presence of Spirit. As one age collapses, a new one begins. One of the tasks of Christians with their many gifts and functions in the pluralistic Mystical Body of Christ is to scout out the future. Where is the Spirit active? Where does God's absence become presence in man and future? This is a task for all of us. It is precisely in this area of living as Christians, of praying and believing, that the theologians and bishops have less to say, and the lawyers and social workers have very much to offer. Christian spirituality has always been marked by a strong charismatic spirit; the theologians of the Christian life ranged from kings and chancellors to lawyers and diplomats, from missionaries to housewives. The following pages simply suggest signs of future directions; they are not meant to suggest "schools of the spiritual life," nor are they in any way complete. Perhaps these directions are meant to offer methodology of discovery. They begin, as they must, from our own times and culture, and go on to ask how Christ emerges out of the very characteristics (which some may have hastily condemned) of this place and time. There are three different approaches here. The first suggests that we try to develop the message of particular writings of the New Testament in order to find out how the gospel is outlined there, and how Mark, John, or Romans suggests a Christian should live. Secondly, I single out two famous men whose writings are among the very, very few which are read today in the sphere of Christian spirituality. Both were primarily involved in the secular world, one as scientist, one as diplomat. Somehow, while Ignatius Loyola and

Francis de Sales and hundreds of lesser figures cannot speak to us, these two men make sense. They are certainly, at least, beginnings. Finally, since both were, at least in origins, Europeans, there is some discussion of American Christian life.

New Testament Theologies

One of the two dimensions of radicalism is the event of Jesus Christ as recorded in the Scriptures. This implies taking seriously the need felt everywhere to discover a biblical proclamation of what Christian community, vocation, mission, and witness mean. Rather than pursue these words in a systematic theology drawn from the entirety of the Scriptures (which is foreign to the New Testament books themselves), let us try to see how they were understood by particular communities, preachers, and theologians of the early Church, for example, by Paul, by Luke, and in the Johannine writings. Although much of the necessary information for this enterprise is available in lexicons and journals, it remains to be applied to the structures and lifestyles of the Church today. Jerome Murphy-O'Connor, O.P., professor at the Ecole Biblique in Jerusalem, has written a study of some of the basic realities of religious life as presented in the theology of Paul's letters.[7] He arranges around them the topic of *witness,* of the individual and of the community.

Christians as individuals have come from darkness to light (Col. 1:12f.). In the midst of the "deceitful" world as "children of God" they are to "shine as lights in the world, holding forth the word of life." (Phil. 2:14–16). "The essential point to note is that the Christian fulfills this function not by saying something but by doing something. It is not a question of the

[7] "Religious Life as Witness," *Supplement to Doctrine and Life,* 17 (1967), pp. 115–142.

verbal proclamation of the Gospel."[8] Preaching for the individual Christian consists in the quality of his life, and this life is the word of life. It is neither composed of distinctly Christian actions, nor of compulsive "good works." Rather, the Christian's life is to stand out as something striking, beautiful, attractive.

Paul was convinced that Christian witness is given within the context of normal social activity. *Good* works due to circumstances may not always be clearly perceived but this is exceptional and in the nature of things cannot endure for long. "Good works are conspicuous, and even when they are not, they cannot remain hidden" (1 Tim. 5:25). They will eventually have their effect. They are the essential Christian witness.[9]

Father Murphy-O'Connor shows at length the interplay of *human* and *Christian* in the life and witness of the Christian.

Even though we conceive our lives as Christians as an imitation of Christ we are rather inclined to forget that the basic lesson of the Incarnation is that *we must become men*. Acceptance of this fundamental point is basic to the idea of witness, for only the activity of fully mature and complete human beings can have the quality on which Paul lays emphasis.[10]

The Christian as witness implies the imitation of Christ. The following of Christ is not so much a slavish imitation of his particular life, but being conformed to Christ, totally imbued with love which will manifest itself in the quality of life. Paul's life is one of re-incarnating Christ.

A witness is someone who happens to be on the spot when something happens and can attest to it. The greater his objectivity the happier everyone is. Not so for Paul. A witness who is not involved is not a witness. In order to justify Christianity as a relevant factor in our world

8 *Ibid.,* p. 118.
9 *Ibid.,* p. 124.
10 *Ibid.,* p. 124f.

we often content ourselves with evoking the memory of the great saints who graced this earth. This is pure escapism. Our efforts to hide behind them only succeed in demonstrating our inadequacy. A Christian who has to point to anyone other than himself to justify the present reality of the love of God in Christ has no right to consider himself an apostle. His whole *being* must proclaim this love.[11]

St. Paul often rejoices in the fact that different communities have been witnesses of faith and love, churches as witnesses to each other. Yet, the Christians of the first decades did not stand out as sectarians in their world. Living in quite different milieus —Greek, Roman, Syrian—they sought to penetrate the social structure through the good works and lives of the individual members of the community. They had and wanted no competition with community pressures, no points of power or influence, no struggle with the secular political order in becoming an "establishment."

A religious vocation does not introduce one into the hierarchy nor does the religious occupy a place intermediate between the hierarchy and the laity. A Christian becomes a religious because he feels that this is the way *for him* to realize the full potentialities of *his* baptism. He remains an authentic layman, and his vocation is only a modality of that of the laity. Hence what the New Testament says of the witness-value of the Christian life in general applies with full force to religious.[12]

Two points in regard to the witness value of religious life are emphasized. It has a mission to provoke through life and action ultimate questions in both believers and unbelievers. Secondly, although there is a place for the monastic and contemplative aspect, the Christian community is essentially an open com-

[11] *Ibid.*, p. 130.
[12] *Ibid.*, p. 134. "If the first chapters of Acts are understood to reflect the pattern which religious life attempts to produce—and in theory they have been—it follows that religious life must be lived in and for the world." *Ibid.*, p. 137.

munity. Luke's sketch of the primitive community in Jerusalem presents its characteristics:

All those who believed lived together and had all things in common, and they sold their possession and goods and distributed them to all, as any had need. And day by day, attending the Temple together and breaking bread in their houses, they partook of food with glad and generous hearts, and singing God's praises and having favor with all the people. And day by day the Lord added to their number those who were being saved (Acts 2:44–47).

This community is open, anxious for dialogue and contact, eager to share with each other, but without any tone of self-preservation or fearful withdrawal. This brief summary of Pauline theology is an indication of the fruitfulness and necessity of turning to the New Testament, to the early Christian communities reflected in the scriptural writings, and turning to them through historical-critical study. They are not just normative, but in a mysterious way perenially liberating and creative.

Faith in the World: Dag Hammarskjöld.

Books have already appeared on the life of the former Secretary General of the United Nations, a life which united many aspects of traditional Christian (to a great extent Catholic) mysticism with a life of public service seen precisely as service, asceticism, and evangelical realization.[13] What is significant about Hammarskjöld is his emphasis of the suffering and ascetical aspects of the Christian life in the midst of the social and political ambitions of New York City and the United Nations. Suffering overcomes fear and selfishness, and gives light, especially as a

---

[13] Henry von Dusen, *Dag Hammarskjöld: The Statesman and His Faith* (New York, 1964); Sven Stolpe, *Dag Hammarskjöld: A Spiritual Portrait* (New York, 1966).

preparation for future service. This Swedish mystic, as *Markings* shows, belongs to the apophatic tradition of Pseudo-Dionysius and the Spanish mystics. He sees grace and service necessarily bound to suffering and darkness. His genius is to live this out in the midst of cocktail parties, embraced loneliness, and bitter public attacks. This theology is secular not in the sense that it is derived from the world, but that Hammarskjöld successfully lived traditional ideas at a profound depth in the midst of new surroundings and professions.

Christians in an Evolving Cosmos: Teilhard de Chardin

When a man walks through the tunnel connecting a jet plane to a large terminal, he moves through thousands of people in an artificial world of television screens, lights, air-conditioning, conveyor belts. A woman gets off a subway or suburban train and when she reaches the street level, she is surrounded by a city of tall buildings and half-completed taller ones, by busses, trucks, cabs, and cars, by hot neon and cool inviting interiors. What sense does all of this make for a Christian, for any human being conscious of a destiny greater than the sum of the secular city? A highly interiorized or subjectivized view of the dialogue between God and man—based exclusively on Protestant justification or Aristotelian faculty psychology, or on the static world of some sixteenth- and nineteenth-century spiritual systems can lead only to frustration. Teilhard de Chardin was concerned with this problem. He wrote: "I would like to be able to have a great love for Christ in the *very act* of loving the universe. Is that a dream or a blasphemy? Besides union with God and union with the world, can't there be a union with God through the world?"[14] This Teilhard took as his principal task:

[14] H. de Lubac, *The Religion of Teilhard de Chardin* (New York, 1968), p. x. See R. Faricy, *Teilhard de Chardin's Theology of the Christian in the*

137

love of God and love of world united, the mutual interpenetration of the Christ with evolving creation. As we now are overwhelmed with a perception of the power and promise of human technology, the rapid pace of humanity rushing toward an unknown future, and the multiplying evils of inhuman use of nature by man, Teilhard is one possible mentor in the Christian life. He saw that because the world is evolutionary and increasingly self-responsible, the previous *patterns* of Christian spirituality would prove to be insufficient. They involved flight from the world and interior quests potentially oblivious of the world.

In its classic and ancient form, the theory of Christian holiness rests on the idea that nature (in contrast to supernature) is complete— fulfilled. . . . Under these conditions, holiness for men cannot consist in anything other than taking flight alone into the supernatural. Anything else is of no interest to the Kingdom of God, except insofar as it is needed, for an arbitrary period of time, to assure that life goes on through the ages. And for this, the children of the world could be enough. Essentially, the Christian is more purely a Christian the sooner he detaches himself from the world, the less he uses creatures, the more he approaches spirit.[15]

What kind of positive view would Teilhard offer?[16] Lack of space and lack of competency forbid any attempt at a full treatment here. What is important is simply to indicate that Teilhard provides a satisfactory and inspiring world view, where Jesus Christ, the Church, the life and potential of Christians makes sense and seems valuable within an evolving tech-

---

World (New York, 1967), pp. 3ff. Faricy contrasts this approach not only with "classical spiritualities" but with the writings of Thomas Merton and Louis Bouyer (*ibid.*, p. 24).

[15] *Note sur la notion de perfection chrétienne* (1942), cited in Faricy, p. 21.

[16] See the books by Faricy and de Lubac already cited along with C. Mooney, *Teilhard de Chardin and the Mystery of Christ* (New York, 1966), and P. Chauchard, *Teilhard de Chardin on Love and Suffering* (Glen Rock, N.J., 1966).

nological world and solar system. The perspective of faith is released from its interior and private sphere. It assumes again the Pauline and Johannine aspects of the real world being influenced by the event of Christ. This event is not the descent of a spectral divinity, but the incarnation of the Word of God.

And it is here, irrespective of all philosophical or theological considerations, that Christianity decisively takes the lead with its extraordinary power of immortalizing and personalizing in Christ to the extent of making lovable the time-space totality of Evolution.[17]

The historicity and humanity of God's definitive word tells us to value our own time and culture. For so long the churches were afraid of progress, discovery, and improvement because they felt these would be used against them: either to render them obsolete or to disprove their dogmas. Now it is possible with Teilhard's help to reverse this situation, and to see mankind as within a Christian milieu, not that of the medieval world but of a cosmic forward process. It has God as its source and destiny, with the God-man Jesus Christ as its moving center. Daringly and with uncanny precision Teilhard describes our age as both intellectually sophisticated and searching: "Whatever may be said, our century is religious—probably more than any other. How could it fail to be with such vast horizons opening before it and with such problems to be solved? The only thing is that it has not yet the God it can adore."[18] Faith then adds a deeper perspective; it does not fear or preclude the evolving secular one. It can both rejoice in and criticize man's city and satellites. There is room and need for Jesus Christ at the pulse of humanity, and the Christian's vocation is one not only of ambiguity but of challenge: to under-

[17] *The Future of Man* (New York, 1968), pp. 208f.
[18] C. Cuénot, *Teilhard de Chardin* (Baltimore, 1965), p. 368. This passage helps to form the theme of CBS News' film study of Teilhard, Bonhoeffer, and Buber: *Roadsigns on a Merry-Go-Round*.

stand and to work for the Kingdom of God as it is described in the synoptics, immanent and transcendent vis-à-vis the world.

We now have many theologians of hope, but Teilhard has formulated the crucial question. It carries further the ambiguity of the Kingdom of God, and asks: What is the relationship between the positive resolution of history and creation in the Parousia of Jesus Christ, and our efforts on earth to build a better world? For Teilhard they are directly related. The negative version of this idea is not foreign to us: that we prepare for punishing destruction by our sins. The positive vision is more challenging. God's providence is incarnational even to the point of fulfillment, so that man's efforts for a better world and society allow the diffusion of grace and peace, and so prepare for the positive resolution of history. The Christian catalyst working with and within innumerable secular groups and movements is the Christian *ecclesia*. Its source and its contribution is love, the blood stream of what Teilhard calls hominization.

Christian charity, which is preached so fervently by the Gospels, is nothing else than the more or less conscious cohesion of souls engendered by their communal convergence *in Christo Jesu*. It is impossible to love Christ without loving others (in proportion as these others are moving towards Christ). And it is impossible to love others (in a spirit of broad human communion) without moving nearer to Christ. Hence automatically, by a sort of living determinism, the individual divine *milieux,* in proportion as they establish themselves, tend to fuse one with another; and in this association they find a boundless increase of their ardour. This inevitable conjunction of forces has always been manifested, in the interior lives of the saints, by an overflowing love for everything which, in creatures, carries in itself a germ of eternal life.[19]

These ideas are neither dogma nor system, and must be balanced with other factors such as sin and the possibility of cosmic

[19] *The Divine Milieu* (New York, 1960), p. 44.

disaster. They could be carried further into Teilhard's views of the important roles of the Church and the eucharist.[20]

For Teilhard the creative operation of God is not an activity which happened once, with pieces to be picked up at the eschaton, nor has it molded us like clay to be impressed by powerful nature and history. Rather man becomes master of nature and history. Man should give himself to God's creative action, understand it, work with it.

It is through the collaboration which he stimulates in us that Christ, starting from all created things, is consummated and attains his plenitude. . . . We may, perhaps, imagine that creation was finished long ago. But that would be quite wrong. It continues still more magnificently, and at the highest levels of the world. . . . And we serve to complete it, even by the humblest work of our hands. That is ultimately, the meaning and value of our acts. . . . With each one of our *works,* we labor—in individual separation, but no less really—to build the Pleroma; that is to say we bring to Christ a little fulfillment.[21]

Man does not bring about the eschaton, but through God's plan, the final maturity of mankind into peace coincides with the second coming of Jesus Christ (who is God and man) in a single event.[22]

[20] See Faricy, *op. cit.,* pp. 129–137; Teilhard, "The Mass of the World," and "Christ in the World of Matter," *Hymn of the Universe* (New York, 1965), pp. 13–59.

[21] *The Divine Milieu,* p. 56; see Faricy's sections on this book, pp. 101–129; pp. 173–209.

[22] "The collective effort of human evolution cannot by itself bring about the Parousia. That mankind reach a point of maximum maturation is, in Teilhard's evolutionary framework of thought, *not* a sufficient condition for Christ's second coming. It is, however, a necessary condition. . . . Teilhard has no intention whatever of denying the gratuity of God's intervention in the world at the end of time, of denying the gratuity of the Parousia. Christ's second coming could never be brought about merely by the powers of natural evolution and human effort. The Parousia is a supernatural event. What Teilhard does deny is that the Parousia will be an *arbitrary* event, unconnected with human evolutionary progress." Faricy, p. 211.

Christians in America

Dag Hammarskjöld and Pierre Teilhard de Chardin direct us to the United States. The Swedish diplomat entered a new world when he came to New York as Secretary General of the United Nations and it was in New York that he experienced his greatest suffering and insight. It is the United States which most obviously reflects the vision of Teilhard: the possibility of world-wide charity and communication through technology; the union of world and Church focused on the future. In the past five years European theologians have also shifted the spotlight to the United States with their call for a political theology. Such a political theology cannot just pay lip service to political metaphysics; it must be born of contemporary political experience. This experience is pragmatic, social affluent, technologically successful and revolutionary. Like American theology, an American spirituality must develop out of this experience of being an American. It must interpret life, grace, and service in dynamic functional terms.

American Christian life will be highly community-oriented as technology produces alienation and threat. At the same time it will recognize that human life is increasingly involved in ecology, in human and/or artificial environments. The "floating parishes" are attempts at creating religious environment without leaving the world, without creating an artificial, heavenly environment of a pseudo-gothic church or a chapel filled with long-dead saints. America is functional and pragmatic—its serving cannot be separated from prayer; the old divisions into contemplation and action collapse before the intermingling of prayer and action. When is a protest march a liturgy? Why is prayer, at times, possible during active service and impossible in quiet rectories or sanctuaries? Prayer must be discovered within the very act and life of ministry, just as theory

142

in America is seen and verified in production. The American will not expect new static, once-and-for-all methods of spirituality to appear; rather, he will see that his own faith and service must go through different periods of evolution. Some of them can be seen as levels of personal maturity but all of them will involve a great deal of uncertainty, since our own future is uncertain. Will America's social problems be solved? The answer to this question is a purely sociological one, but has repercussions for faith and prayer. American spirituality cannot escape being pragmatic. An extreme interpretation of this would be to expect verification of the dialogue between person and grace (perhaps some Pentecostals seek this unbelieving, pragmatic verification of the Spirit in their lives). On the other hand, we cannot expect meaninglessness and aridity, neurosis or paranoia, selfishness and unhappiness to be, as they once were, tolerated for years under the promise of a heavenly reward— when they could be cured or eliminated through a change of scene. What is the role of contemplation and silence, of solitude in American spirituality? Monks and nuns are not the only Americans who recognize the need for silence amid the sounds of tearing down and building, amid the upheavals of anger and neurosis. But this solitude may of necessity be compartmentalized. There is a "contemplative backlash" present now in the renewal of religious life, a recognition and preparation for solitude and silence, for places of retreat. Still, this must be one period in religious life; a "mixed life," both active and contemplative, is very difficult to sustain. It is difficult because the apostolate in our world is so demanding. The mixed life frequently failed, because it was intrinsically impractical and overbearing.

It would be possible to develop a kind of American theology of "holiness" around figures such as Martin Luther King, the Kennedys, certain student activists, victimized soldiers in Vietnam, civil rights leaders. The names would all be controversial, and controversy is so lacking from most of our hagiography of the ancients. It seems that contemporary forms of American dedication and service exist mainly in groups. This indicates the tremendous role that community and the search for it plays in our society. At the risk of appearing outrageous, let us allow two groups to stimulate our ideas on Christian spirituality: the hippies and the student activists.

THE HIPPIES' SEARCH

Paradoxically, at a time when Catholic monastic communities are going through an identity crisis that questions the value of their vocation itself, groups of young Americans are building and living contemplative community in, what for lack of a better words, are called "hippie communes." Simply outlining the intentions and characteristics of these communes is striking. They are a protest against the materialism and hypocrisy of contemporary society in which man is exploited for the gains of business or political status quo. They are active signs of the *possibility* of peace among men. They involve a radical sharing, although their experimentations have shown the necessity for limitation in areas of sex, children, living space. They are an affirmation of the goodness of nature—from flowers to physical love.

This movement raises some serious questions for religious life. We have here a warning that open secularization and social ministry are not absolutes for the religious life. They must be submitted to another standard of religious values. As contradictory as it may appear (and as much as our unbalanced novitiate experiences may militate against this), silence, prayer, thought, contemplation, and communion with nature, the deepest values of the Benedictine and Cistercian life are still ultimate. Are not the hippie communes also a protest against the increasingly

144

rapid and worldly character of even religious life? It is en-couraging to see a "contemplative backlash" growing among religious communities; this includes the establishment of houses of prayer and retreat. The rediscovery of "monastic" and "solitary" values will grow, as we work out of our systems the bad aftertaste of enforced, rigid, unyielding medieval life under the disguise of contemplation.

There is a radical question raised here about openness, crea-tivity, and radicalism. Many monastic communities are ques-tioning not just the *how* of their vocation, but that vocation itself. Too often, their response to this question is to try to bring the contemplative or monastic life *into* the crisis places (seen locally), into the ghetto, usually. This may be one partial solu-tion, but it must be recalled that now the "mixed" orders have finally had the honesty to recognize that it is impossible to combine the monastic life with a twentieth-century apostolate. It is impossible to live like Carthusians and at the same time run a high school for the 1970's. Is not the entire concept of leaving the monastery for the inner city, or moving it to the ghetto, a typical principle of false "renewal"? It is the quick, but also the easy solution. It appears radical, but it is not radical enough. Over against it stands the phenomenal interest of the young in Eastern religions, in communes, in the free university with its concomitant communal living, in nature and quiet, in drugs (as a sacrament of vision, contemplation, escape). There is something wrong here, if the great Christian monastic tradi-tions feel they must end their history while ignoring this re-birth. But to be open to this movement demands going deeper than renewal, local change, liturgical adaptation. It implies a risky openness of the monastery to the world as it is. Con-templation and prayer, typically monastic values of the cycle of seasons, attention to nature would have to be taken *as they are*. They could not be swiftly transformed or labeled or dismissed according to values from the thirteenth or nineteenth century.

145

The monastery would become a center for those interested in these values. It would offer the way of Christ, a way with great depth, a way which affirms incarnationally the value of the individual without opting for a negation of the Word of God through purely human experiences of drugs or human introspection which might close off God's action. Naturally this involves risk, because our world is risky; it involves patient witness and Christian discovery; it involves ministry. In the last analysis, however, this is no more or less than what Christian life and ministry will have to be; the necessary dialogue with the world in apostolates moving from century-long sameness to rapid change, from obsolescence to newness.

STUDENT ACTIVISM

The growing number of politically activist students take seriously the value of the individual person, especially in his struggle not to be exploited by big business, the industrial-military complex and self-aggrandizing politicians. They reflect the evangelical message of the primacy of each person consecrated by Christ.[23] The New Left is critical of the hypocrisy and ultimate pessimism found now in all politics. "Their [Democratic Party liberals'] themes purport to be different but always the same impressions emerge: Man is inherently incapable of building a good society; man's passionate causes are nothing more than dangerous psychic sprees . . . ideals have little place in politics . . ."[24] Carl Oglesby has stated that New Left politics is essentially a moral movement. In the charter of the SDS Tom Hayden writes: "Making values explicit is an activity that has been devalued and corrupted. The conventional moral terms of the

[23] See Michael Novak, *A Theology for Radical Politics* (New York, 1969).
[24] Thomas Hayden, "A Letter to the New Left," *The New Student Left*, M. Cohen and D. Hale, editors (Boston, 1967), p. 4.

age, the political moralities ('free world,' 'peoples' democracies') reflect realities poorly, it at all, and seem to function more as ruling myths than as descriptive principles."[25] What are the values espoused here? Again, it is the primacy of the person over questionable institutions that do not work too well, a hope to improve the future, the realistic and idealistic option for what have always been impossible human and political situations—world peace, incorruptible justice, and so on.

We regard *men* as infinitely precious and possessed of unfulfilled capacities for reason, freedom, and love. We oppose the depersonalization that reduces human beings to the status of things. We oppose, too, the doctrine of human incompetence because it rests essentially on the modern fact that men have been "competently" manipulated into incompetence. . . . Men have unrealized potential for self-cultivation, self-direction, self-understanding, and creativity. It is this potential that we regard as crucial and to which we appeal—not to the human potentiality for violence, unreason, and submission to authority. The goal of man and society should be human independence: a concern not with image or popularity but with finding a meaning in life that is personally authentic; a quality of mind not compulsively driven by a sense of powerlessness, nor one which unthinkingly adopts status values, nor one which represses all threats to its habits. . . . This kind of independence does not mean egoistic individualism; the object is not to have one's way so much as it is to have a way that is one's own. Nor do we deify man—we merely have faith in his potential. Human relationships should involve fraternity and honesty. Human interdependence is contemporary fact; human brotherhood must be willed, however, as a condition of future survival and as the most appropriate form of social relations.[26]

We can only wonder if all of the police, mayors, judges, and university presidents with whom the student activists have come into conflict have thought out and arrived at the same ideals.

These movements attract tens of thousands of young people

25 "Port Huron Statement," *The New Student Left*, M. Cohen and D. Hale, editors, p. 10.
26 *Ibid.*, pp. 11ff.

147

willing to suffer physically and socially for them, while the religious life has much less impact. What inspiration can we draw from this? First of all, religious communities must allow a significant fraction of their members to become actively involved in the various movements struggling for peace, racial equality, state and local justice, political independence. Religious who are called to this should be supported, encouraged, not just tolerated. Secondly, we can learn here about mobility. One of the guidelines of these movements is not to set up permanent institutions. These goals and causes may last a few months, may last a few years. Mobility and adaptation and the perseverance to move from one difficult situation now improved to another one must be cultivated. Thirdly, religious groups should become the core of movements (not the controllers or leaders) and attract groups of auxiliaries. Many young people wish to work for social improvement and for the Christian Kingdom, but not over a lifetime. It may be the future of the religious to be mobile core groups, enabling through experience and Christian independence changing groups of people to work for the ambiguous Kingdom of God, coming and already present.

There is a strange view, present within religious communities as within the churches as a whole, that peace is effeminate, that injustice and conflict are normal, that political and judicial and military corruption is impossible. This must be exorcised. It is intellectually and politically naïve, and before the gospels either silly or heretical. The gospels themselves support more the directions of political change than of the status quo. They have more to do with the passage quoted above than with decorated generals or foolish Irish politicians. In brief, it is of the utmost importance in this time of great and perhaps ultimate social crisis, that we understand the "secular spirituality" which is found in the New Left. Equally important are the methods and tactics and goals which they employ in their groups and movements. Should we not expect while acknowl-

148

edging a basic pluralism of approaches within the religious life, that some religious would be *the Christian activists?*

The Risks of the New

It would be contradictory to the spirit of these pages and somewhat ludicrous to end with a little catalogue of new-style vices. Yet, it is important to warn against utopianism, against change and improvement as substitutes for faith. The life of any dedicated Christian is a life of faith. It begins in faith and survives in faith. The total acceptance of the gospel perspective is not the same as mental health or urban improvement. Faith transcends the perspectives of this world by its affirmation of sin (exemplified but not ended in the cross) and of a greater promise (the resurrection of all dead exemplified in the Easter of Jesus of Nazareth). Faith is hard. Perseverance in faith is even harder; dedication—a certain level of intensity of faith in action and channeled life—is hardest yet. Corresponding to faith is charism, the subtle voice of the Spirit. Charisms may seem exciting; actually they are dangerous and inconveniencing. There is nothing dramatic about being assassinated or publicly ridiculed, nothing challenging about living for months in uncertainty.

We must be wary of certain negative phenomena developing in religious life. The threat of loneliness resulting from technological and secular change is very severe for religious. While faith is important here, it is not the remedy for loneliness. The importance of community, of independent responsibility and professional future has to be stressed. There is a kind of "voyeurism" among many religious. They have been emancipated, given freedom and some financial means. They have not, however, become more dedicated apostles, but have become watchers of the social scene. They are not doers but watchers;

149

they are not really involved Christians but find their contact with the contemporary society through films, plays, music, a variety of friends. Secondary means have become ends. The danger is that freedom in the religious life will not end in dedication and sacrifice, but in fun! Thirdly, it is already being shown that religious life is not the same as unmarried professionalism. Having an interesting, well-paying, job, even connected to the Christian apostolate, in an interesting place with a stimulating recreational environment—this may be an intermediate reaction to excessive monasticism, but it is not religious life. There are many things it might be, but it has *mistakenly eliminated rather than radically renewed freedom, poverty, dedication and above all community*. Utopianism, humanism, voyeurism, individualism, bachelorism, isolationism—these make a strange list, different from the old sins of pride, ambition, uncharitableness. They are the problems facing the new directions of the religious life. They return us to our original question—the absence of God. The two ways of coping with this absence, under the Spirit and in the power of the Incarnation, reflect love of God and of neighbor. They are unavoidably part of the quest and life of every man: faith and people.

8. Conclusion

The preceding pages have been an encounter between the basic currents of our times and a Christian institution—the apostolic community. Most of the problems, insights, and conclusions gained thereby could be transferred to other ecclesial institutions. The problems faced now by the religious life are the same as the basic questions before all churches. It is not that, for instance, sisters are uniquely embroiled in difficulties; rather, they are ahead of the others (Protestants and Catholics) in facing, or being forced to face, these issues.

The same factors just singled out—secularization, social change, pluralism, person and community, communication—could be the broad model for a constant framework of American ecclesiology. This study of the Church would begin with the exigencies of a New Testament *ecclesia* and move through an American localized network of communities to models for ministry-in-community. The procedure would be much the same as that just undertaken; this indicates that the religious community is one microcosm of the Church, sharing its destiny and future.

Radical questions have been asked; few answers have been given. Those who might have expected the sensational have been disappointed. Yet, the basic and most beneficial answer has been given—a framework within which to think creatively. In the Church as in society, the greatest problem is not one of dogma or morality or authority. It lies deeper. We have a great

151

lack of thinking. For the Christian, thinking Christ is called theologizing. This thinking lies between the poles of God's self-communication in Christ and a particular personal and social situation.[1] As long as we cannot think, we are not free to respond creatively to the awesome demands of history and the joyful ones of the Holy Spirit.[2] Catholic education has taught some how not to think, or, more complicatedly, how to double-think. These people, many in authority, neither want nor are able to think. For them, thinking is a threat. The philosopher Hegel saw the existential risks of thinking, and what he says of philosophy he means as true of life. "The decision to philosophize casts itself completely into thinking . . . as into an ocean without beaches. All bright colors, all mainstays have vanished; all friendly lights otherwise present are extinct. Only one star still shines, the inner star of spirit. It is natural that, since we are alone, our spirit is assailed by dread. It is still unknown where everything will lead, where we will end. Among the things vanished are many which one would not surrender at any price. But in this solitude they have not yet been reconstituted. And it is uncertain whether they will be found again and given back."[3]

Martin Heidegger writes of the need for thinking in our society, echoing the fears of Erich Fromm that we will become slaves of our own unthinking ossification.

The breadth of all growing things which rest along the pathway bestow world. In what remains unsaid in their speech is—as Eckhardt, the old master of letter and life, says—God, only God.

But the message of the pathway speaks just so long as there are men (born in its breeze) who can hear it. They are hearers of their origin, not servants of their production. In vain does man try with his plans to bring order to his globe if he does not order himself to the message

---

[1] Paul Tillich, *Systematic Theology*, I (Chicago, 1951), pp. 3–18.
[2] See Martin Heidegger, *What Is Thinking?* (New York, 1968).
[3] *Berliner Schriften* (Hamburg, 1956), p. 19f.

152

to bring order to his globe if he does not order himself to the message of the pathway. The danger looms that today's men are hard of hearing towards its language. They have ears only for the noise of media, which they consider to be almost the voice of God. So man becomes distracted and path-less.[4]

In our particular spheres of possibility we must learn again—without fear or guilt—to think and to act creatively. St. Paul's letters announce that the Christian is free because he is in a new creation with a goal and purpose. For St. John, to know the truth is to be free, and to know the truth is to do the truth. The radicalism of Christ was not in doing many transitorily shocking things, but in normal settings to associate with the poor and despised, to eat with the wayward, to invite a rich young man or a prostitute to become part of the present yet ambiguous kingdom. It would be a shame if religious life in America followed Europe down paths which seem uncertain and unfruitful. This is all the more true, since it can honestly be said that religious life has never been in as favorable a situation as it is today. The tumult is a sign of life . . . but only if it signals the incarnation of something new and human.

[4] Martin Heidegger, "The Pathway," *Listening*, 2 (1967), pp. 89–90.

Bibliography

Bamberg, C., O.S.B. "Ordensleben als kritische Diakonie," *Geist und Leben,* 42 (1969), 17–35.

Benz, R., B.V.M., Sage, R., B.V.M. eds. *Self-Study for Renewal: Final Reports* (B.V.M.) Dubuque, 1969.

Biot, F. *Communautés Protestantes.* Paris, 1961.

Cardegna, F., S.J. *The Future of Religious Life.* Informal remarks to the Major Superiors Conference, June, 1968: Mimeo.

Cegielka, F. *All Things New: Radical Reform and the Religious Life.* New York, 1969.

Dolores, Sr. M. *Creative Personality in Religious Life.* New York, 1963. Bibl.

Dyer, R. J. *The New Religious.* Milwaukee, 1967. Bibl.

Gaboury, P., S.J. "The Secular Religious and Pluralism," *Review for Religious,* 28 (1969), 604–615.

Grollmes, E. *Vows but No Walls.* St. Louis, 1967.

Heijke, J. *Renewal of Religious Life: Taize.* Pittsburgh, 1967.

Hinnebusch, P., O.P. *Religious Life: A Living Liturgy.* New York, 1965.
————— *Salvation History and the Religious Life.* New York, 1966.
————— *Signs of the Times and Religious Life.* New York, 1967.

Hinnebusch, W., O.P. *The History of the Dominican Order,* Staten Island, 1966.

Kavanaugh, A. "Community and the Liturgy," *Renewal through Community and Experimentation* (CLSA Workshop—Dubuque, 1968), 3–11.

Kruse, R. J. "Religious Life and the Modern World," *Sisters Today,* 38 (1966), 105ff.

Lègasse, S. *L'appel du riche.* Paris, 1966.

Martelet, G. *The Church's Holiness and Religious Life.* St. Louis, 1968.

Matura, T. *Célibate et communauté.* Paris, 1967.

Moran, G., Harris, M. *Experiences in Community.* New York, 1968.

Murphy-O'Connor, J., O.P. "Religious Life as Witness," *Supplement to Doctrine and Life,* 19 (1967).

Murray, G., S.J., "The Secular Religious," *Review for Religious,* 26 (1967), 1047–1055.

Novak, M. "The New Nuns," *A Time to Build.* New York, 1967.

O'Meara, T. F., O.P., ed., "Community and Commitment," *Review for Religious,* 28 (1969), 541–551.

———— "Apostolate and Community: Secularization and Revolution," *Sisters Today,* 40 (1969), 335–346.

Oraison, M. *The Celibate Condition and Sex.* New York, 1967.

O'Rourke, K., O.P., "Spirit, Law and Community," *Renewal through Community and Experimentation* (CLSA Workshop—Dubuque, 1968), 165–176.

———— *Canon Law for Religious Women.* Dubuque, 1961.

Orsy, L., "Charisms and Community," *Renewal through Community and Experimentation* (CLSA Workshop—Dubuque, 1968), 107–115.

Philippe, P., O.P. *The Ends of the Religious Life According to St. Thomas Aquinas.* Rome, 1962.

Predovich, N. *The Challenge of Radical Renewal.* New York, 1968.

Rahner, K. "The Charismatic Element in the Church," *The Dynamic Element in the Church* (New York, 1964).

———— "The Theology of the Religious Life," *Religious Orders in the Modern World.* Westminster, 1966.

———— Various essays in *Theological Investigations*—III Baltimore, 1967.

Ranquet, J. G. *Conseils évangéliques et maturité humaine.* Paris, 1968.

Reichert, K. "Secularization and Renewal," *Review for Religious,* 27 (1968), 552–570.

Richardson, Herbert, "The Symbol of Virginity," *The Religious Situation—1969,* D. R. Cutler, ed. (Boston, 1969), 775ff.

Rousseau, O., "Communauté ecclésiale et communauté monastique," *Maison-Dieu,* 51 (1957).

Ruether, R. "Ministry and the Eschatological Ethic," *Cross Currents,* 18 (1968), 149–158.

Sacred Congregation for Religious "Instruction on the Renewal of Religious Formation," *Review for Religious,* 28 (1969), 335–372.

Scannell, M., O.P. "Meaning in Religious Life," *Sisters Today,* 40 (1968), 7–12.

156

Schillebeeckx, E., O.P. "Das Ordensleben in der Auseinandersetzung mit dem neuen Menschen und Gottesbild," *Ordenskorrespondenz,* 9 (1968), 108ff.

———— *Celibacy,* New York, 1968.

Sexton, W. "Principles of Organization," *Renewal Through Community and Experimentation* (CLSA Workshop—Dubuque, 1968), 22–31.

Tihon, P. "Religious and Secularization," *Religious Brothers in the Church and World Today,* Brussels, 1967.

Visioni attuali sulla vita monastica. Montserrate, 1966.

Walgrave, V., O.P. *Dominican Self-Appraisal in the Light of the Council.* Chicago, 1968.

Weigert, A. J. "A Sociological Perspective on the 'Secular Religious,'" *Review for Religious,* 27 (1968), 871–879.

Wulf, F. Einführung in das Dekret über die zeitgemässe Erneurung des Ordenlebens. Münster, 1967.